BERNADETTE

Produced at the Lauriston Hall, Edinburgh, on 26th August 1958, with the following cast of characters:

(in the order of their appearance)

MOTHER JOSEPHINE IMBERT, Superior of the Mother House of the Sisters of Charity at Nevers	*Viola Keats*
LOUISE SOUBIROUS ⎫ Bernadette's parents	*Joyce Carpenter*
FRANCOIS SOUBIROUS ⎭	*Hugh Evans*
LOUIS BOURIETTE	*Eugene Leahy*
TOINETTE SOUBIROUS, Bernadette's sister	*Catherine George*
JEANNE ABADIE, a school friend	*Patricia Morton*
BERNADETTE SOUBIROUS	*Carol Wolveridge*
M. LACADÉ, Mayor of Lourdes	*Nicholas Tannar*
MME LECLERC, the Dean's housekeeper	*Molly Veness*
ABBÉ PEYREMALE, Dean of Lourdes	*Hugh Ross Williamson*
MOTHER MARIE-THÉRÈSE VAUZOU, Mistress of the Novices at Nevers	*Viola Lyel*
MARIE-VERONIQUE ⎫	*Margaret Ford*
MARIE-HEDWIGE ⎬ Novices	*Marylou Stewart*
MARIE-RAPHAEL ⎭	*Kitty Fitzgerald*

The Play directed by GORDON CRIER
Settings by STANLEY MOORE

THE SCENES

ACT I   The Cachot. A disused prison in Lourdes—February 1858

ACT II   The Dean of Lourdes' study—six weeks later

ACT III   The Convent at Nevers—the Infirmarian's Office—between 1866 and 1879

(The LIGHTS *are lowered twice during Act III to denote the passage of time)*

AUTHORS' NOTE

History has generously provided the
events and characters of this play;
but the play makes no claim to be
anything more than—just a play.

ACT I

In the darkness many voices can be heard singing the Lourdes Hymn. As the LIGHT grows we see a Nun. The sound of the singing increases as a procession approaches and passes; and then slowly fades. The Nun is MOTHER JOSEPHINE IMBERT.

REV. MOTHER. Carrots! Why should I think of carrots? Carrots are asses' food. You dangle carrots in front of donkeys to make them trot. Nuns eat carrots too. At one time carrots were almost the staple diet of our convent. Well, they were cheap, and they were good for us, and . . . And now whenever I hear that hymn I think of carrots. Those are the pilgrims singing it. They come from all over the world to honour Our Lady of Lourdes. And every year it seems to me there are more and more of them, and they come ever more frequently so that my mind is daily filled with carrots. She was good at scraping carrots. It was almost the only thing she could do when she first came to us. We were in two minds then about taking her—of course it's unthinkable now that we should ever have hesitated, but then—well, her health was bad, and she was so ignorant, and it seemed she could do no service to the community at all; and then the bishop asked her what she could do: "Nothing," she said, "nothing at all. I'm good for nothing—but scraping carrots." So, of course, we put her in the kitchen—and carrots became a regular feature of our diet. And now they're talking of canonizing the child. . . . Why? If only we could see each other through God's eyes! How easy it would be to understand.

The LIGHT fades on the Nun.

When the LIGHTS come up again, we are in the Cachot. The building is made of stone, and is dark, damp and cold. A door, up C, leads into a small courtyard. Up L, a curtained alcove with an unusually high step, forms the sleeping accomodation for the children. Below this, in the L wall, there is a fireplace with an old stove that was once used for heating, but now has to serve for cooking—such cooking as the occupants can afford to do; at the moment a pot of soup. Also on the stove is a can of hot water. A rough table with three hard chairs stands in the middle of the room. The only other piece of furniture is a small stool, down R. Farther down R, in the corner, is a shapeless heap of cloth—the parents' bedding—which is pulled out in front of the stove at night.

For a moment the room is empty, then LOUISE SOUBIROUS enters from the courtyard with some children's clothes she has been washing and is wringing out. She disposes them round the stove to dry, pausing for a moment to warm her hands. A child's voice is heard from the inner room.

CHILD (*off*) Maman! Maman!

LOUISE. What's the matter?

CHILD (*off*) Maman, I'm cold.

LOUISE (*to herself*) I know. God help me, I know. (*Calling*) You must try to sleep. (*She looks about her, then takes the shawl from her shoulders and goes into the inner room*) There; that's the best I can do. You can have a little hot soup, then you must go to sleep. (*She comes out of the room, goes to the fire, fills a bowl and takes it back into the inner room*)

(FRANCOIS SOUBIROUS *enters from the courtyard. Hearing him* LOUISE *puts her head out*)

(*With disappointment in her voice*) Oh, it's you. (*She goes in again*)

FRANCOIS (*moving down* R) Who did you think it was, the good Saint Nicholas? Not even that benevolent old gentleman would visit a place like this. (*He takes a few small coins from his pocket and regards them in the palm of his hand*)

(LOUISE *comes out of the inner room*)

LOUISE. Ssh! The boys are going to sleep. (*She closes the curtain*) I hoped it was Toinette and her sister.

FRANCOIS. Are they out then?

LOUISE. They've been out all the afternoon. Any luck?

FRANCOIS. Only this. (*He throws the coins on the table*) Don't ask me how I got them. (*He turns away down* R)

LOUISE (*looking at the coins; concealing her dismay*) Where can those children be? (*She moves behind Francois*)

FRANCOIS. Were they alone?

LOUISE. They went with Jeanne. (*She pats Francois' pockets then holds out her hand*)

FRANCOIS. Jeanne?

LOUISE. Madame Abadie's girl.

FRANCOIS (*resignedly giving Louise the rest of the money*) That old . . .

LOUISE. Now, Francois!

FRANCOIS. Well, she is. She's a gossip.

LOUISE (*putting the coins with the others on the table*) She's a good kind woman; and Jeanne's a nice child, and you ought to be grateful to her mother for letting her come here to play with our children. (*She piles all the coins at the upstage* L *corner of the table*)

FRANCOIS. Grateful! (*He sits wearily,* R *of the table*)

LOUISE (*crossing to the stove*) If it weren't for her you'd be having no supper at all.

FRANCOIS (*suspiciously*) Has she been giving you onions again?

LOUISE. You've always liked onion soup. There was a time when you begged me to make it.

BERNADETTE

A Play in Three Acts
on
The Life of Bernadette Soubirous

by

NOËL WOOLF and SHEILA BUCKLEY
based on an original play by Martin Adeson

SAMUEL   FRENCH

LONDON
NEW YORK TORONTO SYDNEY HOLLYWOOD

MADE AND PRINTED IN GREAT BRITAIN BY WHITSTABLE
LITHO, STRAKER BROTHERS LTD, WHITSTABLE

FRANCOIS. Do you know how many times we've had onion soup in the last few weeks?

LOUISE. Yes, Francois.

FRANCOIS. And you honestly mean to tell me you still like onion soup?

LOUISE. Yes, Francois.

FRANCOIS. Even without cheese on the top?

LOUISE. No, Francois.

FRANCOIS. Then what are we arguing about?

LOUISE. I'm not arguing. I like onion soup—with cheese on the top.

FRANCOIS (*interested*) You don't mean you have some cheese?

LOUISE (*laughing*) The old—gossip—gave me a piece—and half a loaf. (*She picks up the half loaf from the mantelpiece*)

FRANCOIS (*rising and crossing to Louise*) Then I take back everything I said about her. I love Madame Abadie.

LOUISE (*shocked*) Francois!

FRANCOIS. And I love you, too. (*He gathers her in his arms and kisses her*)

(LOUISE *responds willingly for a moment, then breaks away from and crosses below him to put the bread on the table*)

Louise, you're a fine, good, beautiful woman—yes, you are—and you're far too good for me. Look what I've brought you to. And you give me onion soup in return. Now, if only we had some wine . . . (*His glance falls on the coins on the table*)

(LOUISE *has already read his thoughts, and quickly drops her hand over the money, gathers it up, and puts it in her apron pocket*)

Of course not.

LOUISE (*moving round the table to the door*) Where can they be, those two girls?

FRANCOIS. There's no need to worry, they'll come back.

LOUISE (*turning on him*) "No need to worry, they'll come back!" How like a man. (*She crosses behind him to the stove*) Don't you mind what happens to your children? Doesn't it concern you they might be lying dead in a field? Have you no feelings?

FRANCOIS. Poor devils! Who knows it might not be best for them if they were. (*He crosses below the table to the chair R of it*)

LOUISE. How can you stand there and say such a wicked thing? You should be struck dumb. God knows what is best for them, not you.

FRANCOIS. Does He? I sometimes wonder. (*He sits*) What can our daughters expect of this life? Toinette and Bernadette, what sort of men are going to take them for wives without a dowry? What can I give them?

LOUISE. There are other things besides money.

FRANCOIS. Lots of things. But you need money to buy them.

LOUISE. Do you know why I married you, Francois?

FRANCOIS. Why? Because I was a good miller and you hoped I'd make lots of money for you to spend. I was a good miller, wasn't I?

LOUISE (*crossing above the table*) Yes. Yes, you were a good miller. But I loved you, Francois, because . . . (*She puts her arms round his neck from behind, and rests her cheek against his hair*) I'm not good at putting these things into words . . . I wanted my children to be your children—yours, and not any other man's. Can you understand that? I know you can't give them money or any of the things money can buy, but you have given them one gift—something that no-one else could ever have given them. Yourself. And that is something very precious to me.

FRANCOIS. You talk as though you were happy.

LOUISE. Happy? I believe I am.

FRANCOIS. Well, I'm not.

LOUISE. I think the children are too, in their own way.

FRANCOIS. How can a man be happy when he's denied the work God made him for?

LOUISE. You'll feel better when you've got some hot food inside you. We none of us know what work God made us for, and it's no use moaning about it.

(LOUISE *crosses behind the table to* L)

FRANCOIS. I went down to the mill today.

(LOUISE *is stopped by this remark. She looks at him with mingled pity and regret*)

Yes, I've so little pride left I even went to our old mill to beg for work. (*He is about to take a piece of bread*)

LOUISE (*stopping him*) That's for the children. (*She continues to the stove and fills a bowl with soup*)

FRANCOIS. I've crawled to them, haven't I? I'm ready to do a day's work, any work. They just laugh in my face. Swine!

LOUISE. Quiet, my darling. You'll wake the boys and then they'll complain of the cold and . . . (*For the moment her feelings get the better of her*) and then I'll never get them off to sleep again. (*She crosses above the table and puts the bowl of soup in front of him. Then she goes to the door and looks out*)

FRANCOIS (*after tasting his soup*) Aren't you having any soup? It's good, very good.

LOUISE. I'll have mine later; with the children. (*Coming to the chair above the table and sitting*) Francois, I'm worried about them, I am really. I know something's happened. Couldn't you go out and look for them? Now. Go now.

FRANCOIS. What now? Before I've finished my soup?

LOUISE. Well, I shall have to go then. You don't care what

happens to your children so long as you can sit there and fill your belly with hot food.

FRANCOIS. Fill my belly! Ha! Who told me to eat the soup?

LOUISE. I hate you. It's freezing out, and I haven't a shawl.

FRANCOIS. Just now you said you loved me.

LOUISE. So I do, but I hate you also.

FRANCOIS. Where is your shawl? You haven't sold it?

LOUISE. No, no. It's on the boys' bed.

FRANCOIS (*about to rise*) I'll get it.

LOUISE (*stopping him*) You'll do nothing of the kind. You'll wake them up. (*She rises and goes to the door*) I'll go without it. It doesn't matter . . .

FRANCOIS (*authoritatively*) Louise! No harm can come to the children. If it had we should have heard long ago. There are plenty of people who know them.

LOUISE (*turning to him; L of the door*) Something has happened. I know it, I can feel it.

FRANCOIS. Very well, I'll go. (*He rises*) You sit down and rest yourself. I'll be back with them in no time. I'll finish my soup later. (*He hands her his bowl*)

(LOUISE *takes the remains of the soup, crosses to the stove and empties it back into the pot.* FRANCOIS *goes to the door. Outside is* LOUIS BOURIETTE. *Once a stone-mason,* LOUIS *has, for many years, been unable to carry out his trade through blindness. He has so far mastered his infirmity that, although he uses a stick and has sometimes to feel for a piece of furniture, even his friends often forget his lack of sight, and to look at him one would not know it. Well known in the locality he receives small commissions that have so far kept him from actual starvation. Even so there is nothing dirty or unkempt about him, and although he refers to himself on occasions as "a beggar" he resolutely refuses to beg—if he did he would probably look worse and fare better*)

Louis!

LOUIS. Good evening, my friend, good evening.

FRANCOIS (*to Louise*) It's Papa Louis. Welcome to the Palais Soubirous.

LOUISE (*going to the door*) Come in, Papa. Come in and warm yourself. (*She leads him to the chair L of the table*) Have you had anything to eat?

LOUIS. I've done well enough, thank you, well enough.

LOUISE. That means you've had nothing. (*She sits him down and fills a bowl with soup*)

LOUIS. And this might well be a palace, for all my eyes can tell me.

FRANCOIS (*coming behind the chair above the table*) Then you're lucky, if you've lost your nose too, for that would tell you a very different story.

LOUIS. Do I detect a note of bitterness in my old friend?

Louise (*handing Louis the bowl*) Take no notice, Papa, he's had a hard day and he's tired.

Louis. Soup! You shouldn't give it to me. You will be wanting it for the children when they get home.

Louise. There's plenty for them. This is some that Francois couldn't finish. (*She gathers up some pieces of aired laundry*)

(Francois *opens his mouth to protest*)

He's just going out.

Louis (*misunderstanding; hopefully*) Going out? Have you done well today? I have a little something I saved from yesterday, shall we go together and cheer each other?

Louise (*crossing below the table to the chair* R *of it*) No, Papa. He's not done well, and he's going out to look for the children. They should have been home long ago and I'm worried. (*She puts the laundry on the table*)

Louis. Then if that's all you have to worry about that's all right. They're coming.

Louise. You've seen them?

Louis. They've been down to the river to look for bones. It's a long way; they'll be home soon.

Francois. Then I can finish my soup.

(Louis *silently extends his soup-bowl*)

Francois. No, no. You finish that. I'll help myself to more.

(Louise *is about to protest, but* Francois *quietens her with a gesture, goes to the stove, makes a slight noise with the bowl and the pot and then takes the empty bowl to the table where he sits in the chair above it*)

Louis. This soup is as good as a banquet. Better in fact. People who go to banquets have always had too much to eat. They cannot appreciate good food like we can with our empty bellies. I do not hear you eating your soup, friend Francois.

Francois. Then you must be growing deaf, friend Louis. My wife says I am the noisiest eater of soup in Lourdes.

Louise (*not unkindly*) Chatter, chatter. If you're not going to look for the children you can at least do some useful work. Hold these. (*She puts some garments in front of Francois*)

Francois (*holding up a garment*) What's this? I've never seen you wearing these before; and I hope I never shall.

Louise. That's enough of that. If you must think about what you're doing you can keep your thoughts to yourself. And don't make them dirty. If Madame Bolland doesn't get her washing first thing in the morning there'll be no money, and then there'll be no food for any of us.

Francois. Does Madame Bolland wear these? Well, well!

Wouldn't she be surprised if she knew I knew! Do you think her husband knows?

Louise. He's been dead these twenty years, so either he knows everything or else he doesn't care.

Francois. Would you marry a woman who wore things like these, Papa Louis? Fine material, very fine, but no—no *je ne sais quoi!* Just look at them. I ask you!

Louis. You forget, my friend, I cannot see them.

Louise. I'm sorry, Louis, you must forgive him. You manage so well without your eyes—it's a compliment for us to forget.

(Francois *folds the garments*)

Louis. Thank you, but that is one compliment I would willingly forgo. I don't ask much, but I would dearly like to have my sight back—just for a few hours before I die. I'd like to see the friends I've made. I'd give a great deal for that.

Francois. And I'd give a great deal to see your face when you saw some of them.

Louise (*rising and collecting the folded garments*) If it's God's will, I believe you'll have your wish. (*She crosses behind Francois and Louis to the stove and puts down the garments*)

Francois. Take my advice and stay as you are. If it weren't for your blindness nobody would give you a single sou. You haven't four hungry children to feed and clothe; four hungry children with cold, pinched bodies, looking at you with love and trust in their eyes. What have they done to deserve a father like me?

Louise. Hush, Francois, hush!

Francois. I will not hush. What sort of God is He who makes children suffer for the sins of their fathers? They trust me, they think I'm everything a father should be—because they know no better—and I can't even give them toys. I'm the one that's condemned them to living in this hovel, this stinking cess-pit that's not fit for a stable.

Louise. It's not your fault, my darling.

Francois (*rising*) And they forgive me! (*He moves away* R)

Louis. Our Lord was born in a stable, and in poverty. God knows what He's doing.

Francois (*turning back*) Does God know what He's doing when He makes my Bernadette lie awake all night coughing? This cold damp place with its stone floors is killing her; and I can do nothing. And you worry about her, too, Louise, it's no good pretending you don't.

Louise. I do worry, it's quite true. She's a good girl and a great help to me. She looks after the younger ones, Papa Louis, and without her I could never get a day's work done, but for all that I sometimes wonder . . . She can't even read—at her age!

Louis (*chuckling*) What of it? I can't either—even at mine.

LOUISE. Don't joke about it. Everybody loves her, I know; but there are those who shake their heads—and I know what they're thinking—a sick body may be the sign of a sick mind.

LOUIS. That is a wicked thing to say about my little Bernadette. I have never seen her, you know, but when I listen to her voice I can hear something different in it, something I don't hear in other voices—a sort of goodness—that's it—a great goodness.

LOUISE (*crossing to* R *of the table with more linen to be folded*) I wish Sister Marie-Michel could hear it. She says the girl is slow and lazy and won't trouble to learn.

FRANCOIS. Sister Marie-Michel is a . . .

LOUISE. Francois! (*She quickly folds the linen*)

FRANCOIS. All right, I won't say it. But you can't stop me thinking it. She oughtn't to get angry because Bernadette is slow. It isn't right. Nuns shouldn't have tempers.

LOUIS. If she knows her rosary and can say her prayers, what does book learning matter? Do you know I can see more into her heart without my eyes than you can with your two pairs. I think God has looked upon Bernadette with favour.

LOUISE. Papa Louis, you talk too much. Are those things dry yet round the fire? When Madame Bolland's things are finished, there are the children's clothes. Wash, wash, wash, all day long.

LOUIS (*leaning over and feeling the clothes*) They're dry. And I must be on my way. (*He rises*) You're sure you won't come too and cheer me up? (*He moves towards the door*)

LOUISE. He's no spare sous for that kind of cheer tonight.

FRANCOIS. You're an old rascal, Papa, putting temptation in my way . . .

TOINETTE (*off*) Maman! Maman! Look what we've got. Look at the wood.

LOUISE. The children at last! (*She goes swiftly to the door and stands just outside it*)

JEANNE (*off*) We've brought lots of wood, Madame Soubirous. Where shall we put it?

TOINETTE (*off*) We've been all the way to the river. There's lots and lots of wood. We've been very, very good, haven't we? Aren't you pleased with us?

LOUISE. Leave it out here now. Your father will put it away later.

FRANCOIS (*moving to Louis*) Father will do it. Always father! It's not fit for a dog to be out, let father go.

(*They both laugh and move down* R *of the door*)

LOUISE. Look at your clothes! Look at them. Oh, children, children! Really! As if I hadn't enough to do. What your mother'll say, Jeanne, I don't know. She'll never forgive me for sending you home like this.

FRANCOIS (*to Louis*) She'll never give us another onion.

(*They both laugh*)

LOUISE. Come inside at once. I'll have to get you clean some-how. (*She comes* C *above the table*)

(TOINETTE *runs in and comes above the* R *end of the table.* JEANNE *enters and comes to the upstage* L *corner of the table*)

TOINETTE. Is there any supper? I'm awfully hungry. (*She is about to snatch a piece of bread*)
LOUISE (*without malice; slapping her hand*) Wait, you're not the only one.

(BERNADETTE *appears in the doorway. She has a basket under one arm, and comes slowly into the room. Nobody notices her, except* PAPA LOUIS, *who appears to be following her with his eyes—if that were possible*)

JEANNE. I'm sorry, Madame Soubirous, we didn't notice the time.
TOINETTE. You'll never guess where we've been, Maman. We've been miles and miles and miles.

(FRANCOIS *crosses to the door*)

LOUISE. Where are you going, Francois?
TOINETTE. They're cutting the trees down in Monsieur Lafitte's meadow.
FRANCOIS (*taking the basket from Bernadette*) Into the courtyard.
LOUISE. You're not to go outside—in the town—not tonight. Please.

(BERNADETTE *moves down* R)

TOINETTE. Maman, Maman, I'm trying to tell you.
FRANCOIS. I'm going into the yard to wash.

(FRANCOIS *goes out*)

LOUISE. Calm yourself, Toinette, calm yourself.
JEANNE. Don't be cross with her, Madame Soubirous, she's tired and Bernadette . . . (*She sees Bernadette looking steadily at her and breaks off*)
TOINETTE. We nearly went there, but Bernadette wouldn't let us, so we went down to the river instead. We crossed the canal and walked all along the bank to the end. The water was ever so cold.
LOUISE. The water? What water? What's been happening, Bernadette? Haven't you been looking after them?
JEANNE. It wasn't Bernadette's fault, Madame Soubirous, really it wasn't.
LOUISE. What wasn't Bernadette's fault? Will you children talk one at a time. Now tell me, what water was cold? The canal?

TOINETTE ⎫ ⎧ Not the canal, Maman, the river.
JEANNE ⎬ *(together)* ⎨ We had to take our shoes off to cross
⎭ ⎩ the river.

LOUISE. One at a time. One at a time. Listen; sit down all of you. Sit down. Bernadette, give them some bread, while I help out the soup. (*She takes the linen from the table, crosses below the table to the stove, and puts the linen down*)

TOINETTE. Soup! Good, good, good! (*She moves* R *of the table*)

(BERNADETTE *moves between Toinette and Jeanne*)

LOUISE. Perhaps if your mouths are full you won't be able to talk so much. (*She fills two bowls*)

(LOUIS *moves down* R *to the stool*)

TOINETTE (*sitting* R *of the table*) We went to that funny old cave by the river. Jeanne threw her shoes across, but I carried mine.

(JEANNE *sits above the table*)

And the most extraordinary thing happened . . .

(JEANNE *kicks Toinette under the table.* TOINETTE *shuts up immediately and looks at* BERNADETTE *who is offering her a piece of bread. She takes the bread and stuffs a large piece into her mouth.* LOUIS *sits on the stool down* R)

TOINETTE. We didn't go inside, it was all dark and spooky. But we found some bones as well as the wood.

(BERNADETTE *offers Jeanne some bread, but she refuses it. Then she sits* L *of the table*)

LOUISE. Here's your soup. Have you no manners? Since when do you not say good evening to a guest? (*She puts two bowls on the table between Jeanne and Bernadette*)

(JEANNE *and* TOINETTE *now notice Papa Louis*)

JEANNE. Good evening, Papa Louis. (*She passes a bowl to Toinette*)

(BERNADETTE *takes the other bowl*)

TOINETTE (*getting out of her chair and bobbing him a curtsy*) Good evening, Monsieur Bouriette. (*She sits again and drinks her soup*)

LOUIS. "Monsieur Bouriette." That's good. Good evening, Mademoiselle Toinette. Since when has a beggar in Lourdes been called Monsieur?

(LOUISE *crosses to* JEANNE, *who rises, and attempts to to clean up her clothes*)

TOINETTE (*rattling it off*) Sister Marie-Michel told Bernadette that all older male persons should be called "Monsieur" and all older female persons should be called "Madame", unless they are

unmarried and then they should be called "Mademoiselle".
That's manners!

LOUISE. Is it also manners to talk with your mouth full?

LOUIS. So they do teach you something at school, eh? Monsieur
Bouriette! That's good. Very good! I like that. But I'll let you
into a secret, little one, shall I?

TOINETTE. A secret? (*She jumps down and sits on Louis' knee*)

LOUISE. Finish your supper, do.

TOINETTE. It's all finished, Maman. Tell me. Tell me. I love
secrets.

LOUIS. Between you and me, I think I prefer to be called
"Papa". I think "Papa" sounds more friendly, don't you?

TOINETTE (*slightly disappointed*) Yes, Papa Louis.

LOUIS. Between friends we like to know we mean something
to each other. So as a mark of special favour I'll let you call me
"Papa" for always and always.

TOINETTE. For always?

LOUIS. For as long as you remember me.

TOINETTE. I'll never forget you. Never. (*She gives him a quick
hug, jumps down and runs to the table*) Is there any more for supper?

LOUISE. It's time you went to bed. High time. Bernadette,
take her outside and wash her. There's some hot water on the
stove. And you can wash the bowls at the same time.

(TOINETTE *picks up her bowl and runs out.* BERNADETTE *rises,
with her bowl, takes the can of hot water from the stove and follows more
slowly*)

LOUIS. She is excited, little Toinette. You see how life seems
good to her. Everything is an adventure in her world—good and
bad alike. They are wiser than we are, little children, they don't
look always for the reason, for the distress and the heartbreak
that lie behind. For them an event is either good or bad in itself;
the one they enjoy, the other they forget as quickly as they can.
We could learn a lot from them.

LOUISE (*to Jeanne*) You'd better be getting home to your mother
She'll be worrying.

JEANNE. Yes, Madame Soubirous. (*She crosses to* R *of the door,
and stands there hovering*)

LOUIS. But Bernadette, my little Bernadette, *she* is no longer a
child.

(FRANCOIS *enters*)

She is growing up. How old is she now?

FRANCOIS (*crossing up* L) Thirteen.

LOUISE. Fourteen.

FRANCOIS. Well, what's a year or two? (*He comes down to the
chair* L *of the table and sits*)

LOUISE. A lot at her age. I should know.

LOUIS. I will tell you something; do you know, when I am with her it is as though I had my sight again; I can almost see the world, through her eyes.

JEANNE. Monsieur Soubirous . . . (*She comes down* R *of the table*)

FRANCOIS. Yes?

JEANNE. If one makes a promise one must keep it, mustn't one?

LOUISE. Really, Jeanne, this is no time to start an argument.

FRANCOIS. Yes, Jeanne. A promise should never be broken.

JEANNE. Even when someone has made you promise something you won't want to do?

FRANCOIS. Even then. It's a solemn undertaking made in God's name. To break it would be to break faith with Him.

JEANNE. But if somebody else . . . Oh, it's so difficult.

LOUISE. What is all this nonsense? Either tell us quickly or go home to your mother.

JEANNE. It's so difficult, Madame Soubirous.

LOUISE. It's not something to do with Bernadette, is it?

(JEANNE *is silent*)

Jeanne Abadie, if it's anything to do with her you must tell me at once.

JEANNE. I promised her. It's so difficult.

LOUISE. I'm her mother. I have a right to know. Is she ill? Did she have a fit of coughing when she was out?

JEANNE. No, no, it's nothing like that at all.

LOUISE. Then what is it? I insist on knowing.

LOUIS. Jeanne. Jeanne, come here.

(JEANNE *moves to* L *of Louis*)

LOUISE. Papa . . .

LOUIS. Ssh! It is wrong to tell a lie, isn't it?

JEANNE. Oh, yes.

LOUIS. But you know there are little white lies that we all tell and that most of us pretend not to notice, without which life would be quite unbearable. Even Monsieur Soubirous told one tonight. He pretended to take some soup to put me at my ease, but that lie will be forgiven him because he only meant good by it. Bernadette is older than you, yes, but she is still young, and it is not always for her to know what is best. So I think you should let this be one of those little "white" promises that do not always have to be kept.

LOUISE (*impatiently*) You've heard what Papa Louis said, now tell us . . .

FRANCOIS. Louise! Sit down and take it easily.

LOUISE. How can I take it easily. You have no feelings, any of you.

Louis. I think you should sit down . . . she will tell us, but in her own time.

Jeanne. It will not be wrong if it will help her?

(Louise *sits above the table*)

Louis. It can never be wrong to help other people.

(Jeanne *moves up* r, *wrestling briefly with her conscience*)

Jeanne. Well, it was when we were crossing the river—we looked back to see if Bernadette was following, but she wasn't, she was on her knees with her rosary.

Louise. I can't think why she should have been, but that doesn't seem . . .

Francois (*putting a hand out to check Louise*) Go on.

Jeanne. We called to her but she didn't answer. Then she asked us if we'd seen anyone, and when we said we hadn't she said it didn't matter and made us promise not to say anything.

Louise. Well, really, if that's what all the fuss is about . . .

(Bernadette *appears in the doorway. She stands there unobserved by the others, listening.* Louis *rises and backs a step down* r, *his head turned towards Bernadette*)

Francois. Let's get this clear. You were down by the river . . .

Jeanne. By the cave . . .

Francois. The cave at Massabielle?

Jeanne. Yes, we saw some bones on the other side, and I threw my shoes across. We looked back . . .

Louise. We?

Jeanne. Toinette was with me. Bernadette was still throwing stones into the water.

Louise. Throwing stones?

Jeanne. To see if it was shallow enough to cross without having to pull her skirt up. She'd told us we shouldn't do it—the water was up to our knees.

(Bernadette *moves slightly into the room,* l *of the door, as* Toinette *runs in past her to Louise*)

Toinette. Must I go to bed, Maman?

Louise. Quietly! (*She sits Toinette on her knee*)

Jeanne (*seeing Bernadette*) I'm sorry, Bernadette. Indeed I am. I had to tell, really I did. I know I promised but I couldn't help it.

Bernadette. It's of no matter. (*She crosses to the stove, and stands there, withdrawn*)

Toinette. Did she tell you how cold the water was? It made my legs go all goose-pimples.

Louise. If you want to stay you must be quiet. What happened then?

JEANNE. Toinette and I went on. Then we looked back and saw her—Bernadette—on her knees with her rosary.

TOINETTE. You called her "goody-goody" . . . you said, "She's good for nothing but saying her prayers."

JEANNE (*coming down stage* R *of the table*) I didn't mean that, Bernadette. Really, I didn't.

LOUISE. Of course not. Go on.

FRANCOIS (*rising*) It all sounds like rubbish to me.

JEANNE. We called to her, but she didn't seem to hear us. She didn't answer, then I threw a stone. I didn't mean to hit her, I was only trying to attract her attention, but . . . but she still didn't move.

FRANCOIS. You mean to say the stone hit her, and she didn't move?

JEANNE. I think so.

FRANCOIS. Where?

TOINETTE. On the shoulder. It was a big one. I saw it. I should have cried.

(FRANCOIS *turns to Bernadette, and either rolls up her sleeve or pulls aside the neck of her blouse to see her shoulder, first the right then the left, as he does this he passes her across towards the table*)

FRANCOIS. Louise . . .

(LOUISE *puts* TOINETTE *down and comes* L *of Bernadette and looks at her shoulder*)

LOUISE (*under her breath*) Holy Mother of God! I must put something on it. Why didn't you say when you came in?

BERNADETTE. No. (*Gently she disengages herself and crosses below the table*)

FRANCOIS. Leave her alone for now. It won't do any harm; the skin isn't broken.

JEANNE (*as she passes*) I didn't mean to hurt you, Bernadette. You know I didn't.

BERNADETTE. Of course not. It's nothing. (*She moves* L *of the stool*)

LOUISE. Francois, what's it all about? I don't understand.

JEANNE (*moving* C *below the table; to Bernadette*) You do forgive me, for hurting you and for telling them?

BERNADETTE. There's nothing to forgive. It doesn't matter.

TOINETTE. Tell them about the girl.

LOUISE. The girl? What girl? (*She moves below the chair* L *of the table*)

FRANCOIS (*crossing above the table to the right end of it*) You haven't mentioned a girl before.

JEANNE. Tell them what you told us.

(BERNADETTE *is silent*)

LOUISE. What did she tell you, Jeanne?

JEANNE. When she caught up with us . . .

TOINETTE. She said the water wasn't a bit cold, though it gave me . . .

FRANCOIS. Ssh!

TOINETTE. We had to crouch down and rub our legs to get them warm.

FRANCOIS (*raising his voice*) Will you keep quiet?

TOINETTE (*cowed at last*) Yes, Papa . . .

FRANCOIS (*to Jeanne*) Where did you meet this girl?

JEANNE. We didn't meet anyone. We didn't even see her. It was Bernadette . . .

FRANCOIS (*to Bernadette*) Did you see a girl?

BERNADETTE. Yes. (*Every time she thinks affirmatively of her lady the joy of it is reflected in her voice*)

FRANCOIS. Someone you know?

BERNADETTE (*shaking her head; barely audible*) No.

FRANCOIS. You've no idea who she was?

BERNADETTE. No.

LOUISE. Didn't the others see her, too?

BERNADETTE (*after looking at Jeanne and Toinette for a moment*) No.

FRANCOIS. You saw her and they did not?

BERNADETTE. Yes.

FRANCOIS. But you were with them when you saw her?

JEANNE. We were on the other side of the river. But there wasn't anyone in sight anywhere. I'm sure.

BERNADETTE. She was in the cave—high up. The wind rustled the branches and—she was there. (*She is reliving the wonder of it*)

FRANCOIS. What did this girl say to you?

BERNADETTE (*after a pause*) Nothing.

FRANCOIS. She didn't speak?

BERNADETTE. No.

FRANCOIS. What did she do then?

BERNADETTE. She smiled.

FRANCOIS (*incredulous*) Smiled? Was that all?

(BERNADETTE *is silent.* FRANCOIS *crosses to Louise and shrugs his shoulders*)

LOUIS (*coming forward*) Bernadette, this girl of yours, she was beautiful?

BERNADETTE. Oh, yes!

LOUIS. Tell me. Help me to see her.

BERNADETTE (*moving close to him*) Of course, Papa Louis. You know the cave . . .

LOUIS. The Grotto we used to call it. Yes, I remember it. And up above there is a little cave inside . . .

BERNADETTE. That's where she stood. High up—above my

head—where the brambles are. I had to rub my eyes several times—but she was still there smiling. I think she wanted me to go nearer—but I *dared* not move.

Louis. Dared not?

Bernadette. Oh, no! (*Utterly practical*) If I had she might have gone away.

Louis. And how was she dressed?

Bernadette (*seeing it all again*) In white. All in white. Everything about her was white.

Jeanne. You told *us* she had a blue girdle.

Bernadette. A blue girdle, yes. And there was some gold, too—the chain of her rosary—and on her feet . . . But, oh, Papa Louis, her smile!

Louis. Thank you, Bernadette. Thank you.

Bernadette (*in happy wonder*) And she wants me to go back.

Francois. You said she didn't speak.

Bernadette (*not answering him*) I know it. I know it in my heart. And on her feet, Papa Louis, there were roses. A yellow rose on each foot. At first I couldn't even make the Sign of the Cross. My hand wouldn't move.

Louise. Pray for her, Francois. It may be a soul in Purgatory.

Bernadette (*moving L a little*) Oh, no, Maman. I was frightened for a while, yes, but then there was so much light about her and she was so beautiful . . . And when the lady made the Sign of the Cross, I made it, too—quite easily.

Louis. The lady!

Louise (*with a quick move to Jeanne*) Jeanne! Louis! Not a word of this to anyone. Do you hear? Not a word! A good night's rest and she'll be all right in the morning. But for pity's sake not a word.

Jeanne. No, Madame Soubirous, not if you don't want . . .

Louise. Now go home, Jeanne, please. Quickly. (*She passes the girl across her*)

(Jeanne *goes up* L *of the table to the door.* Francois *follows her*)

And you, Papa Louis. I don't want to turn you out, but leave her to us. She'll be all right. We can look after her. A good night's rest and by morning she'll have forgotten all about it.

Francois (*moving down* R; *to Louis*) You'd better go. She wants it.

Jeanne. Good night, Madame Soubirous. Good night, Monsieur.

Louise. Good night.

Francois. Good night. (*He moves up to the door*)

Louis. Young lady, you can take me to the bottom of the road.

Jeanne. Yes, Papa Louis. Good night, Bernadette.

(Jeanne *goes out*)

Louis (*to Bernadette*) Thank you, my child. You've made me very happy. Very happy. (*He goes to the door muttering*) A lady in white—a blue girdle—and yellow roses—a lady in white . . .

(Louis *is gone*)

Louise (*moving* l *round the table to Toinette*) It's high time you were in bed, Toinette. Off you go now and don't make a noise.
Bernadette (*crossing up* r *above the table*) I'll put her to bed, Maman.
Louise. No! No, you stay here. (*She stops her, and puts her hand casually on her forehead*)
Francois. Let her go, Louise.

(Louise *and* Francois *exchange looks*)

Francois. They'll be all right.
Louise. Very well. Run along. And if you wake the boys I'll slaughter you. Quickly now.

(Bernadette *exits to the inner room.* Francois *moves to the chair* r *of the table and sits*)

Toinette (*running to Louise*) Good night, Maman.
Louise. Good night. (*She crosses to the fireplace and lights the lamp on the mantelpiece*)
Toinette (*running to Francois*) Good night, Papa.
Francois (*lifting her on to his knee*) Toinette.
Toinette. Yes, Papa?
Francois. Have you been a good girl today?
Toinette. Yes, Papa. I got lots of wood.
Francois. Then go to bed and dream of all the beautiful things you'd like to do.
Toinette. Can I dream about the doll I saw?
Francois. What doll is this?
Toinette. A huge, huge doll.
Louise. It's one we saw in a shop window last week.
Toinette. It opened its mouth and shut its eyes and said "Maman".
Francois. Yes. You can dream about it. Now off you go. (*He puts her down and gives her a little smack behind*) Oop-la!
Toinette (*gaily*) Good night.

(Toinette *runs into the inner room*)

Louise. Ssh! Quietly. (*She brings the lamp to the table*)
Francois. That's all I can give them, any of them, dreams.
Louise. I do hope she'll be all right.
Francois. Toinette?
Louise (*crossing to the stove*) No, the other. Where did she get it from?
Francois. Do you think she was feverish?

LOUISE. No, I felt her brow.

FRANCOIS. People have had visions before.

LOUISE. Visions! Do you think it was a Holy Vision?

FRANCOIS. Holy or unholy—it could have been. I don't know. I'm not clever enough.

LOUISE. Perhaps we should talk to the priest.

FRANCOIS. You think we should ask him?

LOUISE. I don't know. If we mention it outside these walls . . .

FRANCOIS. Well?

LOUISE (*moving above the table*) Well, don't you see, it's like a shameful secret.

FRANCOIS. Now you're exaggerating.

LOUISE. Well, it is. Already there are some people who think she's not right in the head.

FRANCOIS. Nonsense, she's a good girl. And very helpful. You've always trusted her, and she's never let you down.

LOUISE. Yes, but she's slow, and she can't learn, and . . . Did she really see anything at all?

FRANCOIS. You heard what she said.

LOUISE. Yes, but was there really a girl?

FRANCOIS. If there was the others didn't see her.

LOUISE. Was it just her imagination then?

FRANCOIS. Or a trick of the light perhaps. The sun reflected on the water, making a sort of—halo.

(LOUISE *goes to the curtain of the inner room*)

LOUISE (*calling quietly*) Come in here when you've finished with Toinette. (*Returning to the chair above the table*) You must talk to her again.

FRANCOIS. I must!

LOUISE. You're her father; it's your job. (*She sits*)

FRANCOIS. What can I say to her?

LOUISE. Question her. Find out if there was anyone for her to see.

FRANCOIS (*with sarcasm*) Oh, that's easy. Ask her a few questions and find out.

LOUISE. Ask her to describe the girl again, and if she's different this time we shall know she's making it up.

FRANCOIS. You know all the questions, why don't you ask her?

(BERNADETTE *appears through the curtain. She has brought her mother's shawl, and she crosses to Louise and drapes it over her shoulders. Louise looks up. She takes Bernadette's hand and presses it against her cheek*)

LOUISE. Dear Bernadette. Tell us more about this girl, or lady —or whatever she was.

BERNADETTE. I've told you, Maman. There's nothing more. (*She releases herself and stands between her parents*)

Louise. Are you sure you saw her?
Bernadette. Quite, quite sure.
Francois. Was it a girl or a lady?
Bernadette. A lady—I think.
Francois. You told us first it was a girl.
Bernadette. Did I?
Francois (*triumphantly*) There you are, you see!
Bernadette. She was small, but . . .
Louise. But what?

(Bernadette *is silent, trying to recapture perhaps the scene as she witnessed it*)

Francois. Listen, child, think again. Couldn't it have been that your eyes were playing you? Or perhaps you had fallen asleep for a moment—yes, that's it—you weren't properly awake for a moment, and you had a dream . . .
Bernadette. No, Papa.
Francois. Sometimes a dream can be very real, and afterwards we can't always tell whether it happened or not.
Bernadette (*with frightened almost desperate disappointment*) Can't we? (*She looks from one to the other*)
Louise. Your father is right, you know. It was just a dream.
Bernadette (*sadly*) Was it?
Francois. Of course it was. We know you didn't mean any harm by it, and we forgive you . . .
Louise. But others might not see it in the same way, and it doesn't do any good telling people such stories. It might get you into trouble, you know.
Bernadette. Oh, no. She wouldn't do that.
Louise. Bernadette, there wasn't any lady.
Bernadette (*obediently*) No, Maman.
Louise. You must believe that, please, please.

(Bernadette *is silent*)

Francois. You wouldn't want your mother and father to suffer for anything you had done, would you now?
Bernadette. Oh, no, Papa.
Francois. Then you must forget all about it, and never mention it again. Do you understand?
Louise. Go to bed now. Have a good sleep and we'll hope that in the morning you will have forgotten it all.
Bernadette. Yes, Maman.
Louise. Meanwhile your father and I will pray for you.
Bernadette. Thank you, Maman. (*She crosses towards the inner room*)
Louise. Bernadette.

(Bernadette *stops and turns towards them*)

Aren't you going to say "good night"?

BERNADETTE. Good night, Maman, Papa, good night.

(BERNADETTE *exits into the inner room*)

LOUISE (*worn out*) Well, that's that. Let's go to bed, Francois. (*She rises and puts her chair up stage against the wall*) I thought there couldn't be anything in it. The girl's tired and probably overwrought.

(FRANCOIS *and* LOUISE *move the table up stage.* LOUISE *puts the chair from* L, *above the fireplace, and the lamp on the mantelpiece.* FRANCOIS *puts the chair from* R, *against the* R *wall.* LOUISE *crosses to the corner down* R *and drags the bundle of bedding into the middle of the room*)

We must see if we can't send her away. Perhaps her aunt would have her again. I've had enough for one day.

LACADÉ (*off*) Is this the place? (*Incredulously*) They live here? Well, what can one expect of such people. You wait here.

(*There is a hammering at the door and it is unceremoniously pushed open.* LACADÉ *enters. He is feeling very irritated*)

LACADÉ (*quite unnecessarily*) Which of you is Soubirous? (*To Francois*) Are you Soubirous?

FRANCOIS. What the devil . . . ?

LACADÉ. Now, my man, I don't want any insolence from you. Are you Soubirous? Answer me yes or no.

FRANCOIS. What if I am? What's it to do with you?

LOUISE (*crossing to Francois to restrain him*) Francois! (*To Lacadé*) You must excuse my husband, Monsieur, he's tired and we are just going to bed. Please explain what you want, and then leave us.

(LACADÉ *looks contemptuously at the bedding and skirting it as though it might contaminate him, moves into the middle of the room.* FRANCOIS *makes a threatening gesture but* LOUISE *puts out a hand to restrain him*)

LACADÉ. What is this fantastic tale I hear?

LOUISE. How should we know, Monsieur?

LACADÉ. I won't have this blasphemous tomfoolery, do you hear? You put her up to it, of course.

FRANCOIS. I don't know what . . .

LACADÉ. You know well enough. So does the whole town by now. That blind beggar has been telling everyone. He won't spread any more tales tonight. Your girl'll find herself in jail, too, if she doesn't behave herself. Holy visions indeed!

LOUISE. Oh, no!

LACADÉ. He was paid well enough for the story, I'll be bound.

FRANCOIS. I don't know what Louis has been saying, he has no right . . .

LACADÉ. I'm not having this sort of thing in Lourdes. You will deny it at once.

LOUISE. Of course, M'sieur, we deny it. Bernadette is a good girl. She thought she saw something, but we've convinced her . . .

LACADÉ. It's not her that'll need to be convinced now, it's all those out there. You should be ashamed of yourselves.

FRANCOIS (*advancing on Lacadé*) I've had enough of this . . .

LOUISE (*following him and holding him back*) We've done nothing wrong, M'sieur.

LACADÉ (*showing his distaste of Francois' proximity and retreating down* L) Don't play the innocent with me. Do you think I can't see through your little game? (*Mockingly*) We can't make an honest living, so our daughter shall see visions and we'll be rich.

FRANCOIS (*with another step towards Lacadé*) Get out of here.

LOUISE (*stopping him*) Francois, you'll do no good . . .

FRANCOIS. I may be poor, but if you think I've sunk so low I'll make a peepshow of my child . . . (*He breaks off*)

(BERNADETTE *has come out of the inner room. They all stand looking at her*)

LACADÉ (*quietly*) Are you the girl?

LOUISE. Answer the gentleman, Bernadette. There's no need to be afraid.

LACADÉ. Leave this to me.

BERNADETTE. It's true, what they say. I asked them not to tell, but it's quite true.

LACADÉ. You saw who?

BERNADETTE. I don't know, M'sieur. Just a lady.

LACADÉ. And what sort of a lady is it do you think, that lurks there in a cave?

BERNADETTE (*remembering*) She was beautiful.

LACADÉ. What's that to do with it? Was there anyone with you?

LOUISE. Her sister, and Jeanne Abadie.

LACADÉ. And did they see this—this play-acting?

(BERNADETTE *is silent*)

Did they?

BERNADETTE. No.

LACADÉ (*having caught her in the trap*) There you are! (*Changing his tactics; paternally*) Come here, child.

(BERNADETTE *comes down to him*)

There's no need to be afraid. It isn't your fault. Somebody put you up to this, didn't they? You just tell me it's all a trick, and we'll say no more about it, eh?

BERNADETTE. Yes, M'sieur. I asked them not to tell, but . . .

LACADÉ. That's all right then. Tomorrow you shall come to my office and sign a written denial . . .

LOUISE. We'll see she's there, first thing in the morning. We don't want any trouble, M'sieur.

BERNADETTE (*agonized*) Don't make me, Maman. Please!

LOUISE. But, child . . .

BERNADETTE. I can't deny my lady.

FRANCOIS (*no nonsense*) We'll see she's there, M'sieur.

BERNADETTE. She wants me to go back.

LACADÉ (*his voice dangerously calm*) Who wants you to go back? Where?

BERNADETTE. The lady.

LACADÉ (*through his teeth*) I'll see you in prison first.

FRANCOIS. You mind your tongue . . .

LACADÉ. And you keep your daughter in order, or you'll be in jail, too.

LOUISE (*to Francois*) We'll complain to the priest.

LACADÉ. The priest! Is he going to allow a girl like this to make a mockery of his church? I'll see that he hears about it, don't you worry. And you keep away from the place, understand?

BERNADETTE (*obediently*) Yes, Monsieur.

LOUISE. We'll see she does.

FRANCOIS (*to Louise*) We'll send her to her aunt in Bartres.

BERNADETTE. No, Papa. (*It is a statement of fact*)

FRANCOIS. What do you mean. No? You'll do as you're told.

BERNADETTE (*again it's a fact*) The lady won't let you do that.

LACADÉ (*getting angry*) There is no lady! And if there were, how do you think she could prevent your father? Eh?

BERNADETTE. I don't know. Perhaps . . . Perhaps she'll make papa change his mind.

FRANCOIS. And why should I change my mind?

BERNADETTE (*utterly reasonably*) If I went to Bartres it would be too far for me to walk to her grotto.

LACADÉ (*his temper going*) God give me patience! You're not going to the grotto again, child; not if I have to barricade the place with every policeman in Lourdes.

BERNADETTE. But if the lady tells me . . .

LACADÉ (*with exaggerated patience*) If the lady tells you, you must just disobey her, that's all there is to it.

BERNADETTE. If you'd seen her, Monsieur, you'd never be able to refuse her.

LACADÉ. Well, I haven't seen her, and there is no lady, so the problem doesn't arise.

BERNADETTE (*irrefutably*) If you think there is no lady, Monsieur, why does it matter if I go back?

LACADÉ (*with a cry of fury*) Bring her to my office in the morning. (*He goes to the door and turns, shaking his fist at her*) You'll suffer for this.

The CURTAIN *falls*

ACT II

Scene—*The Dean's study. Six weeks later.*

It is a large airy room, into which the sunlight streams through the glass-panelled door and windows which look out R on to the garden. In the opposite wall, L, a door leads to the hallway. The back wall is covered with books, and there are two or three well-chosen pictures. Near the centre of the room is the Dean's desk; a large flat-topped affair, untidiedly covered with papers, and with a small statuette of the Blessed Virgin on the downstage corner. Behind the desk is a heavy armchair. There are three other chairs in the room, all upright; one by the L downstage corner of the desk, one down R below the garden door, and one in the corner up L.

When the Curtain *rises,* Mme Leclerc, *is putting the feather duster over the Dean's desk. She is a homely outspoken peasant woman, in late middle life. A bell rings off stage.*

Mme Leclerc. There's another of them! All right, I'm coming. (*She moves a heap of papers, dusts under them and puts them back*)

(*The bell rings again*)

All right! All right! You're an impatient one. Can't you wait? There's more important things than opening the door to you. (*She lifts another pile of papers, uncovering a sizable book*) If his Reverence can't find his breviary when he comes in there'll be the devil to pay. (*She picks up the book and places it with an irreverent thump where it can be seen*)

(*The bell rings a third time*)

Ring! Ring! Ring! Who do you think you are? (*She gives the book a deliberate dusting, leaves the duster on it, and crosses L to the door*) If his Reverence were at his prayers you'd get short shrift whoever you may be.

(*By this time she is off and opening the front door. She returns a moment later with* Lacadé *following her. The mayor is more pompous than usual, strutting and excited*)

You can come in. (*She crosses above the desk and recovers her duster*) Father Peyramale will be here directly.

Lacadé. He's out there? In the garden? (*He seems about to go out*)

Mme Leclerc (*coming down* r *of the desk between him and the garden door*) I shouldn't go out to him, if I were you. (*She plants herself as though to resist Lacadé's passage by force if need be*)

Lacadé. I'm in a hurry. The matter's urgent.

Mme Leclerc. He doesn't care to be disturbed, Monsieur.

Lacadé. And I don't care to be kept waiting.

Mme Leclerc. As you please, Monsieur. He'll be very angry; and when he's angry he's most unreasonable. If you've come to ask him a favour it would be better to wait.

(Lacadé *obviously has second thoughts and moves away down* l)

Lacadé (*crossly*) I don't ask favours.

Mme Leclerc (*taking a step towards him*) You've come about the Soubirous, I expect.

Lacadé. I've come on my own business.

Mme Leclerc. They all come about the Soubirous. And it does no good. They get nothing out of him.

Lacadé (*turning*) Nothing? How do you know? Do you listen at the keyhole?

Mme Leclerc. I show them out, and I can see by their faces. Besides the Dean is so worried, poor man. (*She moves below the desk*)

Lacadé. You'd be worried if you had our responsibility.

Mme Leclerc. And if you had mine, Monsieur, you'd be dead. Try looking after Father Peyramale for a week. I've had him for twenty years. To think that a slip of a girl like that could set the whole province by the ears. And a sick one, too. I've seen her when the asthma is on her, fighting for breath; and after she's been at the grotto, sometimes, she's prostrate for hours.

Lacadé (*moving up stage; restlessly*) You've been to the grotto?

Mme Leclerc. I always go when I can. And I've been to the cachot, too.

Lacadé. I'd have expected the Dean to forbid you.

Mme Leclerc. Forbid me? The Dean? (*She laughs*) I'm not one of his curates. I'd like to see him try.

Lacadé (*coming down to her; threateningly*) Then for your own sake I advise you to keep away. And you can tell your friends, too. That's a warning.

Mme Leclerc. You can't frighten me, Monsieur. What can you do? You've tried to put the girl in prison twice, and each time you've had to let her go.

(Lacadé *moves away* l *with annoyance*)

Do you think the bon Dieu is going to let her suffer for doing His work?

Lacadé (*turning back*) His work! You're all the same, you women. (*He sits on the chair* l *of the desk*) The girl's a fraud. There've been others have seen visions, all women, and not so far from here

either, and not so long ago, and they've all been frauds. And this
girl is no exception.

Mme Leclerc. Not all, Monsieur. Not all. When a girl like
this can defy a whole townful of authority there must be something about her. Can you and all your policemen keep her away
from the grotto? No! Have you seen her down there? I have.
She has too much beauty; and the grace of her . . . Even the
soldiers you took from the Château guard were impressed. And
the inspector fell on his knees.

Lacadé. That was—that was politic. He couldn't afford to
offend the crowd.

(*The* Dean *appears at the garden door* r. *He is a huge, gruff, bear-
like man, entirely accustomed to assuming and maintaining the lead in
any situation. At sight of him* Lacadé *rises abruptly*)

Lacadé. Ah! M. l'Abbé . . .

Dean (*decisively*) No.

Mme Leclerc (*bustling the Dean outside again*) Look at you. Stay
where you are. Don't you dare to come in.

(*The* Dean *stands just outside the door while* Mme Leclerc *dusts
him down*)

Lacadé. No? What do you mean no?

Dean. No. M. le Maire, just no.

Lacadé. But you don't know yet . . .

Mme Leclerc. What have you been doing? As if I needed to
ask. Look at your boots. (*She fetches a stick from just outside the door,
and lifting first one of the Dean's feet and then the other, attacks the mud
attaching to them*)

(Lacadé *moves away, below the desk*)

Dean. Experience has taught me that when you address me as
M. l'Abbé, you are about to ask me to do something quite impossible. And so I save you your breath, and say no.

Lacadé (*turning to the Dean*) But, M. l'Abbé, the matter . . .

Dean. You must excuse me. I have been in my garden, as you
can see. And until I have been cleaned up I can discuss nothing.

(Lacadé *moves away down* l)

Mme Leclerc. How you get in such a mess! You should stick
to the paths, instead of trapsing all over the flower-beds.

Dean. I spend a lot of time in my garden. I find it very restful.

(Lacadé *looks at his watch*)

Have you ever seen an importunate flower?

Lacadé. M. l'Abbé . . .

Mme Leclerc. There! You can go in now.

(*The* Dean *enters and stands just inside the door*)

(*She crosses to the door* L, *talking all the way*) It's no use talking to him. He never listens to anyone. I've been on at him for years to keep the place clean and tidy. It's such a simple matter if only one tries. But there! He never listens to a word.

(MME LECLERC *has talked herself out of the room*)

DEAN. Now, M. le Maire, please be seated.

LACADÉ (*not sitting*) M. l'Abbé . . .

DEAN (*moving behind the desk*) My name is Peyramale. My parishioners call me M. le Curé, or Father—though I would hardly expect you to call me that—but you may take your choice. Sit down. And let us hear the worst.

LACADÉ (*not sitting*) This girl . . . something must be done about her.

DEAN. This girl? What girl?

LACADÉ. The Soubirous girl, of course. You must take action. (*He moves restlessly down* L)

(*The* DEAN *leans across the desk and rings a small bell*)

Why do you ring the bell?

DEAN. You have asked me to take action.

(MME LECLERC *enters* L, *almost too promptly*)

Some wine, if you please. (*He sits behind the desk*)

(MME LECLERC *exits*)

Sit down, man, for heaven's sake. Wearing out my carpet will not help you for one moment to keep your Lourdais in order.

LACADÉ (*coming back to the* L *end of the desk*) That's just it. Our people of Lourdes are getting out of hand. I have exercised my authority to the limit, and now it is your turn.

DEAN (*forcibly*) Sit down.

(LACADÉ *sits* L *of the desk.*

MME LECLERC *enters with a carafe of wine, sets it on the table and exits*)

(*As he pours out the wine*) Have you ever stood in a pulpit?

LACADÉ. No.

DEAN. You should try it one day. From there one gets a fine view of the whole congregation. I assure you it requires no great effort of memory to know that an important citizen has not attended mass for several weeks. (*He pushes a glass towards Lacadé*) Have some wine.

LACADÉ. You know my views.

DEAN. Only too well.

(*They toast each other*)

Not so long ago the Inquisition and probably the stake would

have been your lot. Now we live in a more enlightened age—
unfortunately.

LACADÉ. I don't see what all this has to do with . . .

DEAN. Don't you? You have the effrontery to come here and
try to teach me my business as a priest. Why should I listen to a
heretic? Tell me that.

LACADÉ. I cannot see that it is heresy to believe in reason and
knowledge, and to prefer established facts to a pretty fairy-tale.

DEAN. If you believed in God you could never talk like that.

LACADÉ. God! What has He to do with it?

DEAN. Everything. Whenever I am tempted to forget the part
God plays in the forming of this world, I go out there into His
garden, and think on the miracle that is under every leaf, and I
am humble. This town of ours lies in the foothills of the moun-
tains; go up there, in this springtime of the year, and count the
tiny blades of green pushing between the rocks and stones, knowing their long journey through the darkness of the soil will be
rewarded with the light and warmth they seek. If all the knowledge in the world today were at your command, could you order
that mountain-side as God has ordered it?

LACADÉ. Not yet, perhaps. But every day we're learning more
about how "God" works. Already we can go into a darkened
room and say, "Let there be light." We've invented things God
never dreamed of. No, nor the Devil either. How do you think
this town is run?

DEAN. Not without God.

LACADÉ. It's run on hard facts, and the experience of many
years. The experience of men—like me.

DEAN. Facts may serve you well enough in managing your
town, but they are no substitute for God's Church. You deal
with simple things that all men can see and smell and hear and
feel; for you there is no difficulty in making clear your meaning.
The Church has to deal with intangible commodities—Knowledge and Truth; and every now and then it happens that a man
has a new glimpse; something so elusive, so fleeting perhaps, that
it needs a new language to convey it. Until his fellow-men have
learnt that language this new discovery can only be communi-
cated to them by roundabout means—fairy-tales, and reading
between the lines of what I have no doubt you describe as
mystical claptrap. No; do not trouble to deny it; it's of no consequence. Have some more wine? (*He pushes the carafe towards
Lacadé*)

(LACADÉ *refills his glass*)

(*He rises and moves* R) Fortunately Christianity does not rest on
fairy-tales, but on Faith. On Faith and Love and Hope and
Charity. To forgive the unforgivable, that is to be truly Christian;
(*crossing above the desk to* L *of Lacadé*) to hope when all hope is dead;

to love where there is no love to receive in return, and to keep faith in the unbelievable. You like this wine?

LACADÉ. Certainly. It's excellent. Your health.

DEAN. I had it from a grateful parishioner. He had convinced himself that through my agency he was bound straight for heavenly bliss. I should like to believe I may have saved his soul; so much faith deserved to be rewarded. I should also like to think I could help you to an equally happy end.

LACADÉ. Thank you, but I am not thinking of dying yet.

DEAN. That is a most arrogant statement. We are sinners all of us, and I pray that when your time comes you may be lucky enough to be given weeks of sickness in which to prepare your soul—for you will need it; but you would do better not to count on it. Be ready to meet your Maker every minute of the day, for Death may call suddenly and without warning, and he is unrelenting. (*He crosses below the desk to* R) And that reminds me, I am expecting the Reverend Mother from Nevers. You know her?

LACADÉ. I have heard of her certainly.

DEAN (*turning*) Nevers is the Mother House of the Hospice here.

LACADÉ. Is that where the girl's at school?

DEAN. Yes. I've asked her to come to talk about "the girl", as you call her. You shall stay and meet her.

LACADÉ (*rising; hurriedly*) I have to get down to the grotto. She is to be there this morning . . .

DEAN. I insist. I've outlined the Christian virtues to you, now you will have a chance to practice them.

LACADÉ. Really, I should be there. We're expecting a big crowd . . .

DEAN (*crossing to Lacadé*) You came here to talk about Bernadette Soubirous, and now because the Reverend Mother is coming you want to run away.

LACADÉ. I came here to request your help in keeping order in your parish—not to receive a lecture on my problematical soul. What this girl does is as much your concern as mine—if not more. I have a right to expect your co-operation in my capacity as mayor, however much we may disagree as men.

DEAN (*quietly*) You are quite right, of course. (*He turns away down* R) She is my business, and I am deeply concerned, very deeply.

LACADÉ. Then you must use your influence. Forbid these people to go to the grotto, M. l'Abbé. Threaten them with damnation if you like, or bribe them with whatever your Church has to offer, but stop them going.

DEAN (*turning up stage*) Impossible. (*He moves to the window up* R *and stands looking out*)

LACADÉ. They are your flock. They will listen to you. I have done all I can. I have put up barricades, and notices forbidding

them to drink the water; what more can I do? You have never
been to the grotto, you have never seen for yourself the hysteria of
the crowd. At first they came in ones or twos, now since the
spring appeared they crowd there in their hundreds. Soon, if
nothing is done to stop this dreadful exhibition they will be flock-
ing there in their thousands.

DEAN (*quietly*) I know. I am not so ill-informed as you seem to
think, M. Lacadé. (*He turns and comes down* R *of the desk*) Only a
few days ago this child came to see me. It was not the first time,
no; she had been here on several occasions before; and every time
I had been harsh with her; I had tried to browbeat an ignorant
peasant girl, and every time she stood up to me. I believe that
first time there was real fear in that girl's heart, but it did not prevent her from delivering the message she had been sent to give
me. Since then she has been here several times, and each time
she has been less afraid. The last time she came, do you know
what the message was? The Lady wanted people to go to Messabielle in processions, and for us to build a chapel there. (*Turning
away down* R) Oh, I told her the message should have been sent to
the Bishop; that he was the only one qualified to organize a
procession; that the Lady had made a bad mistake in sending her
to me. (*Turning to Lacadé*) And do you know what she answered?
The Lady was not asking us to do anything now, but was expressing a hope for the future. Was that cunning? Or the simplicity of
innocence? Who am I to judge? And why should I be called upon
to do so? One thing I do know; and I am heartily ashamed of it,
I told that girl to go to her Lady and ask for a sign. I told her
that if she were really the person she claimed to be she would
make the briar at her feet burst into bloom.

LACADÉ. And will she ask?

DEAN (*turning up stage; with a shrug of the shoulders*) That I, a
priest of God, teaching others to have faith should have need to
ask for a miracle to convince myself. (*He moves behind the desk*)

LACADÉ (*narrowly*) I think you are on the girl's side.

DEAN. I am on nobody's side but the Church's.

LACADÉ. You have let yourself be fooled by a cheap little
trickster.

DEAN. No.

LACADÉ. Then why will you do nothing? You should be down
there at the grotto guiding your flock.

DEAN (*moving round the* R *end of the desk, to Lacadé*) I don't think
you quite appreciate my position. If I or any one of the priests
under me were to go down there to the grotto, were it only that
we should see for ourselves what went on, we should be proclaim-
ing to the world that the Church gave credence to the stories.

LACADÉ. You can't continue to ignore them.

DEAN. We are not ignoring them. (*Moving round behind the desk*)
Great Heavens, man, do you think your civil power is the only

writer of letters? Look here, and here, and here—documents, memoranda, letters, *to* the Bishop and *from* the Bishop, from priests up and down the country, from gossips, busybodies and people who believe they too have seen visions. Ignoring them! (*He sits*) I tell you when it comes to recording events on paper the Church has the Hotel de Ville knocked into a cocked hat.

LACADÉ (*across the* L *corner of the desk*) Writing letters is not action.

DEAN. Putting one's thoughts on paper is the best way to clarify them.

LACADÉ. And while you sit here clarifying your thoughts, the whole town is running wild. Day after day they break down our barricades; the gendarmes cannot stop them, even the military are powerless.

DEAN. Aren't you trying to make a convenience of the Church? It is not our duty to forbid unless we recognize a real evil, nor is it our duty to exhort and give blessing unless we are convinced the event is genuine. Until we have formed our own opinion in the matter—I repeat our own opinion, and not that of the Mayor and the Inspector of Police—there is nothing we can do. Have you thought of removing your barricades and notices and leaving the whole thing to common sense?

LACADÉ. If the crowds get out of hand . . .

DEAN. According to you they are already out of hand.

(LACADÉ *sits* L *of the desk*)

Have you ever stopped to consider what will happen if Bernadette Soubirous is proved genuine? You'll be no more able to control the flood of pilgrimage than the English King Canute controlled the tide. If, on the other hand, the girl is a fraud—well, she cannot keep it up for ever—the whole edifice of stories will collapse, the people'll go home, and you'll have to take her into protective custody to save her body and I shall have to exert myself to save her soul. Think it over.

LACADÉ (*who has become very thoughtful*) Pilgrims! You think people might come here in pilgrimage?

DEAN (*looking at him*) I did not mean you to make a prophet out of the Dean of Lourdes. But already she has her processions.

LACADÉ. Processions! That rabble!

DEAN. Does it matter whether they march in order like a column of soldiers, or flock like a herd of geese? If the right spirit moves them . . . These people have faith.

LACADÉ. So had the Gadarene swine.

DEAN. I wish I knew.

LACADÉ. You say the Vision asked for a chapel . . .

DEAN. No. I said that was Bernadette's message.

LACADÉ. Is it likely that a church will be built?

DEAN. Is it likely? Great heavens, man, don't ask me. Go to

Tarbes and ask the Bishop, go to Rome and ask . . . I tell you
I know nothing—nothing at all. If this vision is the Blessed Virgin,
if that poor girl proves to be a saint, so far as I'm concerned she
can have three churches. But it doesn't rest with me.

LACADÉ (*almost to himself*) Of course pilgrims would have to
be housed. We should need hotels. (*To the Dean*) Do you realize
what this could mean for Lourdes? Fifty years from now this
medieval fortress could be a great town, ten thousand inhabitants
and a thriving tourist trade. (*He rises and moves down* R) We shall
have to increase the water supply; and the Savy Canal will need
to be diverted; there must be dry access to the grotto; you can't
have visitors getting their feet wet. (*Crossing down* L) And the
processions will need a wide boulevard; yes, I can see it running
straight from the north side of the town to the grotto crossing
the Gave near the Boly Mill—(*turning; to the Dean*) that's most
appropriate—it belonged to the Casterots once—her mother's
family, you know—then it divides and two roads lead to the
church above—that's a fine rock to build your churches on.

(MME LECLERC *enters* L)

MME LECLERC. The Reverend Mother is here, Father.
DEAN (*rising*) Show her in. Show her in. (*He moves* L *of the desk
and crosses below it to Lacadé*)

(MME LECLERC *exits*)

LACADÉ. And souvenirs, too; there'll be shops for selling
souvenirs. I see the new town built north and south of the present
one on lower ground.
DEAN. M. Lacadé, the Reverend Mother is here.
LACADÉ (*coming out of his dream*) Eh?
DEAN. The Reverend Mother . . . You will have to meet her
now.
LACADÉ. Already? She's here now?
DEAN. It's too late for you to escape.

(MME LECLERC *enters and stands above the door.*
The REVEREND MOTHER *and* MOTHER MARIE-THÉRÈSE
enter and come LC. *Mother Marie-Thérèse is an aristocratic and highly
intelligent woman of thirty-three. A martinet, as much with herself as
with those under her, her severe manner often makes her misunderstood,
though in reality she is neither ill-tempered nor unpleasant*)

It's good of you to come, Reverend Mother. You know M.
Lacadé?

(MME LECLERC *takes the chair from up* L *and sets it* L, *and slightly
down stage, of the chair* L *of the desk*)

REV. MOTHER. By reputation. If it was from ourselves that
M. le Maire was wishing to escape he need have no fear. We are

here to discuss the child Bernadette Soubirous I believe, not the running of this town. You know Mother Marie-Thérèse, Mistress of our Novices?

(Mme Leclerc *collects the wine from the table and exits* l)

Dean. Have a chair, Reverend Mother. Make yourself comfortable. (*He indicates the chair* l *of the desk*) And you too, Mother.

Rev. Mother. Thank you. (*She sits*)

(Marie-Thérèse *sits* l *of her*)

Dean. I had hoped Sister Marie-Michel would have been with you . . .

Rev. Mother. That was not possible. This morning she could not be spared from teaching. But you will find Mother Marie-Thérèse well informed about the child. We both visit the Hospice regularly, you know.

Dean. Of course.

Marie-Thérèse. The Soubirous child has been in our care for nearly two years now, Father. She was almost twelve when she first came to our free elementary school. We have had plenty of time to get to know her.

Dean. Then you have the advantage of me. (*He moves above the desk, indicating to Lacadé, in passing, the chair down* r) I have had only one or two visits from Bernadette. Visits, I may say of a rather unusual, if not startling nature. (*He sits behind the desk*)

(Lacadé *pulls the chair forward and slightly up stage and sits*)

I have never known her under more normal circumstances. I have met her parents, true, and decent enough people they struck me; if they are down on their luck; but they may be excused if their judgement in these matters is a little clouded. You, as representing her teachers, should be the ones to give a clear unbiased picture of the girl, one that I can rely on to help me in forming my own opinion of her worth.

Marie-Thérèse. I can tell you her worth in two words; precisely nothing.

Lacadé. Nothing could be clearer than that.

Marie-Thérèse. You agree with me, M. le Maire?

Lacadé (*uncomfortably*) That wasn't what I meant.

Dean. M. Lacadé is undecided whether he wants the girl to be a saint or a charlatan.

Marie-Thérèse. Indeed? Does it matter what M. Lacadé wants? Holy Church is not here to do his bidding.

Dean. He thinks that a saint would be more profitable for Lourdes, but a charlatan would be much easier to handle.

Rev. Mother (*ignoring Lacadé and addressing herself wholly to the Dean*) When Bernadette first came under our charge she was very backward, pitifully backward. She seemed to have been stunted both in body and in mind.

DEAN. Her health is not good, you know.

REV. MOTHER. I do know. Her asthma has kept her away from school on many occasions, too many. Then, she knew the Hail Mary, she could recite Our Father and the Creed. Today, I'm told, she knows very little more.

LACADÉ. Why is that, do you suppose?

REV. MOTHER. Not through any deficiency in her teachers, if that is what you mean, M. le Maire.

MARIE-THÉRÈSE. The reason is plain, she is not only stupid, but lazy into the bargain.

REV. MOTHER. I cannot say we have found her a difficult child, she accepts discipline well enough.

MARIE-THÉRÈSE. Almost too well.

REV. MOTHER. Mother Marie-Thérèse means she accepts it with a resignation that is almost disconcerting.

DEAN. As though, perhaps, she knew it were the will of God.

MARIE-THÉRÈSE. You may call it the Will of God, if you please, Father. In school we know it by another name—dumb insolence.

DEAN (disturbed) I see. (After a moment's thought) You understand, that a very great responsibility lies with us. We have to decide on the facts, and on the facts alone, discounting all emotional appeals, whether they come from others or from within ourselves, whether Bernadette Soubirous is a visionary or not. We are not asked to pronounce on the identity of the supposed vision, nor are we asked whether the girl should be numbered amongst the saints. Those and all other matters are the concern of higher authorities than are to be found in Lourdes. And if now I ask your help, it is because I am determined to form a right conclusion, not only for the sake of the Church but for the sake of the child herself. The Dean of Lourdes cannot go into the highways and by-ways in search of evidence, he cannot enter a public argument without appearing to take sides, without admitting there is something to be argued about. If the Church were to stage a public investigation now, the Church would look very foolish if the whole thing were proved to be a hoax. That is why I must rely on you, M. le Maire, who have talked to the secular witnesses with the help of the Inspector of Police, and on you, Reverend Mother, who have most knowledge of the girl herself. And that is why we must all of us be most scrupulous to be honest with ourselves. M. le Maire, may I have the benefit of your opinion.

LACADÉ (giving his considered opinion) The girl is an impostor.

DEAN. Your reasons, please.

LECADÉ (rising) Consider her history—her family. Her father was no more than a journeyman, a penniless miller who had the good fortune to marry above himself. Why a girl of good family, a Casterot, should choose him . . . Well, there may have been reasons. There have certainly been rumours. At any rate she brought the Boly Mill with her, and he became his own master. And how long did that last? Ten, twelve years, and the place was sold up. And why? I'll tell you why; because Soubirous mère was extravagant, and Soubirous père had no head for business; and so far as I know he has never done an honest day's work since. Have you seen the hovel where they live? If ever you do keep away from the walls and don't sit down. There's an open cesspit right outside the door. Can you wonder the girl's un-healthy? It's a wonder the whole family isn't dead.

Rev. Mother. It's a wonder the Town Council allows such conditions to exist.

Lacadé (*moving to the* r *end of the desk*) If people choose to live in slums—what can we do?

Rev. Mother. They only live in slums because they have no choice.

Lacadé. Are we to build them houses then? Who's to pay?

Dean. Please! We are wandering from the point.

Lacadé. If you try to help them they'll only take advantage.

Dean. Please!

Lacadé (*to the Dean*) It's my belief the girl's been put up to this by her parents. Every time she tells the same story.

Dean. Surely that's in her favour?

Lacadé. In the same words! She's learnt it parrot-wise. It's quite plain to me it's a cheap trick to reinstate themselves in the eyes of the neighbourhood. They hope to get money and work.

Rev. Mother. I don't agree.

Dean. What evidence have you—apart from the girl's?

Lacadé. They're practically starving.

Dean. I have yet to be convinced that starvation is a crime.

Rev. Mother. Not for those who starve, Father, but for those who let them starve.

Lacadé. These people would stoop to anything. They're frequently drunk.

Dean. Have you never been drunk, M. Lacadé?

Lacadé (*turning away down* r) I may have had a little too much wine at times . . . But that is different. Quite different.

Marie-Thérèse. Is it?

Lacadé. Whose side are you on?

Marie-Thérèse. Not on yours, M. le Maire.

Dean. In my simplicity I thought this a straightforward matter of black and white. I see now that I was wrong. There are as many sides as there are people.

(Lacadé *sits down*)

Rev. Mother. I am glad, Father, you are beginning to realize what you are up against.

DEAN. Tell me, M. Lacadé, has this family ever accepted money or other gifts since these visions began?

LACADÉ. Who can tell? It's very probable.

DEAN. My information is that they have not.

LACADÉ. Human nature being what it is . . .

DEAN. Nevertheless the police have failed to prove it. Well, haven't they?

LACADÉ (*grudgingly*) I'm told they've found nothing so far.

DEAN. And it's not for want of trying.

LACADÉ (*jumping up*) That is a most impertinent accusation.

DEAN. Sit down, man. Nobody's accusing you of anything. Sit down.

(LACADÉ *sits again*)

REV. MOTHER. Father, you are making a great mistake. By lending a sympathetic ear you are merely encouraging this girl to further excesses. Believe me I have seen just this sort of thing over and over again. It is very common among the young. For one reason or another a child feels herself inferior to her companions; so she makes an exhibition of herself. It is her way of getting the attention which nature or indifferent parents have denied her. I do not say Bernadette is playing deliberately with people's credulity, it may well be she is unaware of the enormity of her offence; but that does not make the deception any the less monstrous. Nor does it render her any the less liable for the consequences of her behaviour. M. le Maire has asked for action to be taken. It may comfort him to know that we at the Hospice are taking it. While he questions witnesses in his office and while you, Father, with all respect, contemplate the matter here in your study, Sister Marie-Michel is doing all she can to show the girl the error of her ways.

DEAN. How?

MARIE-THÉRÈSE. We have always found, Father, that laughter has great curative properties.

DEAN. You mean she is keeping her amused?

MARIE-THÉRÈSE. I mean the laughter of others.

DEAN. Ridicule?

MARIE-THÉRÈSE. Yes, if you like to call it that, ridicule. That is the best way to cure this unholy exhibitionism.

DEAN (*after a moment's thought; rising*) What you have told me is most disturbing. (*He moves R of the desk*)

MARIE-THÉRÈSE. If we have been able to help you see this matter in its true perspective I am glad. An ignorant slum-girl who claims to have seen the Blessed Virgin . . .

DEAN (*vigorously*) That is not true. She has made no such claim.

LACADÉ. She has said it over and over again. The Inspector has it in writing.

DEAN. I have seen the Inspector's report, M. Lacadé, and there is no word about the Blessed Virgin. I have asked the girl repeatedly for the Lady's name, and she doesn't know. It is you, and you, and the people of Lourdes who have given identity to the Lady of the Vision. I repeat Bernadette has made no claim; on that I will stake my oath as a priest.

LACADÉ. That is the cunning of the child . . .

MARIE-THÉRÈSE. From her descriptions there can be no doubt . . .

REV. MOTHER. You are a good man, Father, given to seeing what is best in other people. It is your nature to overlook their faults; but I pray that you will not let your sympathy for an unhappy child blind you to what is best for Holy Church, and for the girl herself. I tell you if Bernadette Soubirous is not punished for her deception there will be no end to the visions seen in Lourdes. Every disreputable woman of the town will be falling on her knees at the grotto in imitation of her ecstasy.

DEAN. Then you admit hers is real?

REV. MOTHER. I admit nothing. It was a figure of speech.

DEAN (*moving a step below the desk*) Let me ask you one question, both of you: why should Bernadette not have seen a Holy Vision?

MARIE-THÉRÈSE. A girl of her background?

DEAN. And what is wrong with that?

MARIE-THÉRÈSE. Had it been someone who had dedicated their life to the service of God, one might have believed—with proper safeguards, of course.

LACADÉ. Meaning it should have been a Sister of Nevers, I suppose?

REV. MOTHER. Father, I appeal to you . . .

DEAN. Take no notice of the Mayor, Reverend Mother. It has always been the object of the heathen to set us against each other.

LACADÉ. Who are you calling heathen?

DEAN. You are. And you rejoice in it. (*To Marie-Thérèse*) You despise Bernadette because of her simplicity and her poverty. You think that visions should be seen only by holy men and women. May I remind you it was as a poor carpenter and not a priest of God that Our Lord was born.

LACADÉ. This is the nineteenth century. You cannot expect visions and miracles to happen in eighteen fifty-eight. We know how the universe works; what seemed miraculous once has been proved to be the simple ordered workings of nature.

DEAN (*crossing down* L) Because you can give a name to everything, does that mean you can explain it? No. Would it surprise you to be told that you, M. Lacadé, have had a vision?

LACADÉ. I?

DEAN (*turning to him*) Yes. Here in this very room; not half an hour ago. Perhaps not a very holy vision. In fact it was most secular—but a vision nevertheless. I would not presume to compare it with Bernadette's; hers was, I think, inspired by faith; yours by something more material. (*To the Rev. Mother*) It was a vision of a new Lourdes with churches and crowds coming in pilgrimage from the ends of the earth to visit her grotto and bathe and drink the waters of the spring.

LACADÉ. That was—planning—a mere daydream . . .

DEAN. And what is a vision but a sort of dream? Can anyone say where the one ends and the other begins? For some of us our dreams are very real. Can you know for certain that yours will not be fulfilled?

LACADÉ. Frankly I do not believe in miracles.

DEAN. Then I am sorry for you. Truly sorry. For you are wrong. Isn't he, Reverend Mother?

REV. MOTHER. Quite wrong.

DEAN (*moving round behind the desk*) Even in this age there is nothing unusual in the miraculous. It's not the miracles that are lacking, but you that are blind to them. God in the abundance of His generosity, has made them so usual that you no longer recognize them for what they are. How do you know the sun will rise tomorrow?

LACADÉ. Well . . . (*Words fail him, and he seems to be attempting an explanation with his hands*)

DEAN (*coming down to him; gently*) Because it has always done so in the past you think you can work it out by mathematics. But when the sun set on the evening of the first day, how could the world know then that it would ever rise again; except through faith? As day succeeded day that faith grew stronger, feeding on its own belief, until in you, arrogant man, it has become a certainty.

LACADÉ. It would take a miracle now to stop it.

DEAN. And I say it takes a miracle every day to keep it going.

LACADÉ. I'm wasting my time. (*Bustling to the door* L) I should have been at the grotto half an hour ago. (*He turns*) It seems to me it's entirely a matter of how you look at it. But one thing I can assure you—there'll be no miracle down there today.

DEAN. Take care! Even God may not be above temptation.

REV. MOTHER (*to Lacadé*) Who will prevent one? You or your policemen?

LACADÉ. Good day. Good day to you both.

(LACADÉ *exits* L)

REV. MOTHER. It seems to me, Father, there is no more to be said.

DEAN. How simple for you, Reverend Mother, to have no doubts. But then, it's not to you that Bernadette brings her messages. (*Moving the chair vacated by Lacadé closer to the desk, and sitting on it*) When she comes here and tells me her Lady wants a chapel to be built, can I—dare I—ignore it? Oh, if the Lady is a figment of her imagination I must, of course; but suppose she isn't? What then?

Rev. Mother. You think this may be a modern miracle?

Dean. I must know.

Rev. Mother. And you hope God will send you another miracle to tell you to believe it?

Dean. You make it sound like the Devil's work to destroy our faith. (*He rises*)

Rev. Mother. Can we be sure it isn't? Faith must not be confirmed too often, or it ceases to be faith. You are a clever talker, Father, and it is easy to confound the Mayor, but I think God is rightly sparing of His miracles, for they are very terrible. I am more concerned with the welfare of this girl; I understood it was for that reason you asked me to come this morning.

Dean (*moving in front of the desk*) It was indeed. Take her into the convent—at least for a while.

(*The* Reverend Mother *sits for a long moment in silence*)

Rev. Mother. Does the girl wish it?

Dean. She has not asked; but I know her answer. She needs peace from the crowds that follow her, and the understanding of those who have dedicated their lives to God.

Rev. Mother. I cannot promise.

Dean. The child is in grave danger. It's not right she should be pestered; that people should bring her their rosaries to be blessed and clamour to touch her clothing. Since she found the spring in the cave at Messabielle the demands made on her are increasing beyond all reason.

Marie-Thérèse. That was a revolting exhibition.

Dean. It has not seemed so to the people of Lourdes.

Marie-Thérèse. There were those who thought her out of her senses at the time. Really, Father, there is nothing miraculous in grubbing about in the mud and finding water that has always been there.

Dean. She says the Lady directed her to the spot—and she *did* find water.

Marie-Thérèse. She found mud! And she smeared her face with it—like an animal, and nibbled at the grass.

Dean (*turning away* R, *moving round the desk to the chair above it*) That I do not understand, I must confess. But then there is so much . . . But there *is* water now. They say the spring flows strongly. People are bathing in it; and Heaven knows how many have drunk the water—or whether it's fit to drink.

Marie-Thérèse. And has it done them any good? No, Father, the girl has brought all this on herself, and she must suffer for it.

Dean. Suffer! I'm afraid she will. (*After a brief pause*) Let us assume that you are right; let us assume that Bernadette is guilty of the motives you impute to her. (*Moving behind the nuns*) Because she, in her ignorance—you must grant her that at least—if not in innocence—has played with fire, and has loosed upon herself a flood of forces she cannot control, are we to stand aside and let her be swamped by them?

REV. MOTHER. A convent is for those who have a vocation.

MARIE-THÉRÈSE. There are other places she can be sent to for her own protection—the institution or the town jail.

(*Before the Dean has time to reply there is a hurried knock at the door and* MME LECLERC *enters. She is in a state of mild excitement*)

MME LECLERC. The girl is here, Father.

DEAN. Bernadette? (*He moves away, behind the desk and comes down* R *of it*)

MME LECLERC. And there's quite a crowd outside the house has followed her up the road. Both her parents, too.

(*The* DEAN *cannot suppress a sudden elation. He glances at the* REVEREND MOTHER *who, however, does not return his look*)

She is asking to see you, Father.

DEAN. Yes, yes. Let her come in.

MME LECLERC. And her parents?

DEAN. If she wants them, certainly.

(MME LECLERC *goes out. The* REVEREND MOTHER *and* MARIE-THÉRÈSE *rise and stand by their chairs*)

I hope you will stay, Reverend Mother?

REV. MOTHER. If you wish it.

DEAN. At least give her the chance to convince you.

REV. MOTHER (*a little stiffly*) I will keep an open mind.

(MME LECLERC *enters and holds the door open.*
BERNADETTE *enters, followed by* LOUISE, *and* FRANCOIS. BERNADETTE *and* LOUISE *curtsy to the two Nuns.*
MME LECLERC *exits, closing the door.* LOUISE *and* FRANCOIS *drop back and stand a little above the door, the latter slightly up stage. The* REVEREND MOTHER *and* MARIE-THÉRÈSE *sit again*)

DEAN. Bernadette, come here, child. Sit down. (*He moves* R *of the chair* R *of the desk, and offers it to her*)

(BERNADETTE *sits*)

You have been to the grotto this morning?

BERNADETTE. Yes, Father.

DEAN. Those people outside—they were there, too?

LOUISE. They follow her, Father. They never leave us alone.

DEAN. Let her speak for herself.

BERNADETTE. I wanted to come alone, but they followed me.
MARIE-THÉRÈSE. Isn't that what you like?

(BERNADETTE *hangs her head*)

FRANCOIS. Father, you know that's not true. We none of us want them. We can't even be quiet in our own home, with faces at the window and tappings at the door. And when it isn't crowds it's policemen. Tell them to leave us alone.

DEAN. You overrate my powers, Soubirous. They won't listen to me now.

MARIE-THÉRÈSE (*at Francois*) Is it no longer profitable?

(FRANCOIS *takes a step forward, but* LOUISE *quickly puts a hand out to stop him*)

LOUISE. We have never had a sou from anyone. I don't say people haven't offered us money and presents, I can't pretend we haven't been tempted—but we have never accepted anything. Bernadette has forbidden it.

DEAN. Please leave this to me. (*To Bernadette*) Have you any message for me this time?

BERNADETTE. Yes, Father. I told the Lady you had asked for a miracle . . .

DEAN. You did? I'm sorry. And what did she say?

BERNADETTE. She smiled, Father. She is always smiling. She asked again for the chapel.

DEAN. And who is to pay for it? I haven't any money. Have you?

BERNADETTE. Of course not, Father. You know I have none. It's only a small one she wants. It doesn't matter how small.

REV. MOTHER. You say this Lady speaks to you?

BERNADETTE. Yes, Reverend Mother.

REV. MOTHER. Then how is it no-one else has ever heard her?

BERNADETTE. I don't know. She tells me what to do. Perhaps they don't listen as I do.

DEAN. How does she talk? In French.

BERNADETTE (*laughing*) Oh, Father, why should she talk in French to me? She talks as we do at home; like my friends.

MARIE-THÉRÈSE. There you are, Father! As if Our Blessed Lady would talk in patois. How do you explain that?

BERNADETTE. She knows I would never understand French.

MARIE-THÉRÈSE. Ah! So it *is* the Blessed Virgin who appears to you?

BERNADETTE. I never said that, you did. I don't know who she is. She won't tell me her name.

(*The* DEAN *moves quietly up stage behind the desk and sits*)

MARIE-THÉRÈSE. Have you asked her?

BERNADETTE (*turning to the Dean*) You told me to ask her,

Father, and I have. But she only smiles. Today she said something I didn't understand. I've been remembering it all the way
here . . .

Marie-Thérèse. Bernadette.

Bernadette. Yes, Mother.

Marie-Thérèse. This Lady of yours, does she always wear the
same clothes?

Bernadette. Yes.

Marie-Thérèse. And she still has the white roses on her feet?
(*She is deliberately falsifying the information with the object of catching
the child out*)

Bernadette. They are yellow roses.

Marie-Thérèse. This blue dress that she wears, does it come
down to her ankles?

Bernadette. She wears a white dress.

Marie-Thérèse. You told us before it was blue.

Bernadette. No, Mother.

Marie-Thérèse. You are lying, child.

Bernadette. No! It is the sash that is blue.

Marie-Thérèse. Why do you go to the grotto?

Bernadette. That is where the Lady asks me to go.

Marie-Thérèse. Have you never seen her elsewhere?

Bernadette. Never.

Marie-Thérèse. Look—there. (*She points to the statuette of the
Holy Virgin on the Dean's desk*) Is she like that?

Bernadette. Oh, no!

Marie-Thérèse. How is she different?

Bernadette. She is more beautiful. Far more beautiful.

Marie-Thérèse. How long are these meetings to go on?

Bernadette. I don't know. She once asked me if I would do
her the favour of going there for fifteen days . . .

Marie-Thérèse. If you would do her the favour! Presump-
tuous girl!

Bernadette (*turning to the Dean*) What does that mean? Have
I said anything wrong?

Dean. Mother Marie-Thérèse means, I think, that if your
Lady is the Queen of Heaven, the favour is being done by her.

Bernadette. She said it would give her pleasure if I went.

Dean. And what did you say?

Marie-Thérèse (*with sarcasm*) That you would have to ask
your parents, I suppose?

Bernadette. Yes, that is quite right.

(Francois *and* Louise *cannot hide a smile. Even the* Dean *is
amused*)

Dean. Has it ever occurred to you, Bernadette, that this vision
might be evil?

Bernadette. Oh, no, Father!

DEAN. You mean it hasn't occurred to you or it couldn't be evil?

BERNADETTE. She couldn't be. She asked me to pray for sinners, and she promised me . . .

MARIE-THÉRÈSE. What did she promise?

BERNADETTE (*her face shining*) "I cannot make you happy in this world, but in another."

DEAN (*suddenly attentive*) You never told me this before.

BERNADETTE. There are many things she has said that I have not told you, Father.

MARIE-THÉRÈSE. Such as?

BERNADETTE. She has told me things that were for myself alone. That I must never tell anybody.

MARIE-THÉRÈSE. Secrets?

BERNADETTE. Yes.

MARIE-THÉRÈSE. Not even your spiritual adviser?

(BERNADETTE *shakes her head*)

Suppose the Bishop commanded you?

BERNADETTE. He'd never ask me to tell a secret.

MARIE-THÉRÈSE. How can you expect us to believe in your Lady if you won't tell us everything?

BERNADETTE. The Lady never told me to make you believe.

DEAN (*rising*) I think we have asked enough questions for one day. If you have nothing more to tell us, Bernadette, you had better go home. (*He crosses to the garden door and looks out*)

LOUISE (*coming forward to L of Marie-Thérèse*) Come, child. We must brave the crowd again.

(BERNADETTE *rises, moves* C, *below the desk, and curtsies to the Nuns*)

FRANCOIS (*moving above the desk*) Father, you know we don't mean any harm by this?

DEAN (*turning and moving to Bernadette*) I know, my son. Go out by the garden; you'll avoid the crowd.

(FRANCOIS *and* LOUISE *cross above the desk to the door* R)

(*He puts his left hand on Bernadette's shoulder*) Bless you, my child. (*He looks deeply at her*) Though I'm not so sure it is you who are in need of my blessing.

(BERNADETTE *crosses the Dean towards* R)

BERNADETTE (*turning*) What did the Lady mean, Father, when she said, "Que soy l'Immaculade Counceptiou?"

(*For a long moment there is a stunned silence. The* REVEREND MOTHER *and* MARIE-THÉRÈSE *rise*)

DEAN (*to himself*) "I am the Immaculate Conception." She said that to you? Today?

BERNADETTE. Yes, Father. But I don't know the meaning. I repeated it to myself all the way here so that I wouldn't forget it.

MARIE-THÉRÈSE. It's blasphemy, Reverend Mother, that's what it is. Blasphemy! You should be ashamed, child, to put such words into the mouth of this figment. After this we should wash our hands of you.

DEAN (*turning to her*) That, Mother, is something you cannot do. I believe you will live to regret those words.

REV. MOTHER. I think we should go now, Father. I hope our visit has been of use to you.

(*And without another word the* REVEREND MOTHER *and* MARIE-THÉRÈSE *walk from the room*)

DEAN (*moving to Bernadette*) Are you deceiving me, Bernadette?
BERNADETTE. No, Father.
DEAN. What does it mean, "Immaculate Conception"?
BERNADETTE. I don't know.
DEAN. Have you never heard those words before?
BERNADETTE. I don't think so. I don't think so.
DEAN (*rhetorically*) Who has been putting words into this girl's mouth?

(*The* SOUBIROUS *look blankly at one another*)

God help me! I asked and I have been answered, and still I have no faith. (*To Bernadette*) The Lady spoke those words in answer to my question?
BERNADETTE. As you told me, Father, I asked her who she was; I asked her three times. Twice she smiled, and the third time she said—what I have told you.
DEAN. Do you know what day it is today?
BERNADETTE. Thursday of course.
DEAN. Thursday the twenty-fifth of March, Our Lady's Day, the Feast of the Annunciation. And today Our Lady has told you who she is.
BERNADETTE. Has she, Father?
DEAN. My child she who was conceived immaculate, without sin, was Our Lady.
FRANCOIS. Then it's true, Father?
DEAN. True? What is true?
LOUISE. You believe in her?
DEAN. Believe? Does it matter what *I* believe? Let us accept the evidence of our own senses. This much I know: whatever you saw, Bernadette Soubirous, or whatever you thought you saw, it was very real to you. Whether the Blessed Virgin appeared, or whether your vision was a projection of your own great faith, I am sure now that you believe.

(Suddenly the door L *bursts open and* MME LECLERC *enters. She hurries to Bernadette and drops on her knees before the girl)*

Get up, woman. Get off your knees at once. (*He turns away a pace or two towards the door* L)

(In the open doorway stands LACADÉ. *He is very perturbed, but quite unable to express himself, either in words or actions)*

What is all this? Will somebody please tell me what is happening?

*(*MME LECLERC *rises and turns to the Dean)*

MME LECLERC. It's blind Louis, Father. Old Louis Bouriette. He was down at the Grotto . . . and now . . . and now . . .
DEAN. And now what, woman?

(But before MME LERCLERC *can reply* LOUIS *appears in the doorway* L. *He has his stick in his hand, but is not using it, and he stands for a long moment looking into the room. Then he walks steadily across to Bernadette, looking at her the whole time. Arrived there he holds out the stick to her, then drops to his knees and lays it at her feet)*

LOUIS. I went to the spring, Bernadette, I went to your spring, and I bathed my eyes. I bathed my eyes. And I can see.

The CURTAIN *falls*

ACT III

Scene—*The Infirmarian's Office, in the Convent of St Gildard at Nevers.*

The room has two doors, one R *leads to the Infirmary, and one* L, *to the other parts of the convent. A large crucifix hangs in the centre of the back wall, over the empty fireplace. Down* R, *below the door, there is a statue of the Virgin Mary on a bracket on the wall. Up* L, *above the door, there is a cupboard for medical supplies. In the centre of the room a table and three chairs complete the furnishing.*

When the Curtain *rises, the* Reverend Mother *is sitting* R *of the table examining the Infirmary records. At the other end of the table there is a small pile of linen. Also on the table are to be found pen and ink.*

Marie-Thérèse *enters* L *in a state of indignation. She has an opened letter in her hand.*

Marie-Thérèse (*crossing above the table*) Reverend Mother. Reverend Mother, will you take a look at this. (*She holds out the letter*)
Rev. Mother. What is it? (*She takes the letter and reads*)

(Marie-Thérèse *crosses behind her and moves down* R)

She's not the first.
Marie-Thérèse. How the Bishop can let himself be taken in! He should never be sending her to us.
Rev. Mother (*putting the letter on the table*) It is not our task to blame bishops, Mother Marie-Thérèse.
Marie-Thérèse. No, Reverend Mother.
Rev. Mother. And in any case I doubt the Bishop knows anything about it. That's what secretaries are for.
Marie-Thérèse (*turning to her*) Surely the Bishop should satisfy himself the girl is honest in her desire before . . .
Rev. Mother. The Bishop is a good man and holy, but he cannot be more than a man. It takes a woman to search a girl's heart and find out if she has a true vocation.
Marie-Thérèse (*moving in to her*) But this—this is so—so brazen. The girl openly says her only reason for wanting to come here is because we have the Soubirous child.
Rev. Mother. Is that so wrong?
Marie-Thérèse (*turning down stage; with feeling*) Yes, Reverend Mother, it is wrong. Very wrong. If she truly wishes to take the veil it should be for the service of God, not . . . (*She breaks off*)

Rev. Mother. Not what, Mother?

Marie-Thérèse (*evading the issue*) Her motives should be pure. She makes it sound as though having Bernadette Soubirous here were like having a holy relic.

Rev. Mother. Perhaps in that she may only be anticipating the judgement of history.

Marie-Thérèse (*turning to her*) You mean . . . ?

Rev. Mother. I mean nothing. Except that God has many ways of directing our feet on to the right path. The girl who is coming today, the one from Rouen; I accepted her because I thought she had the makings of a good nun. I could not refuse her because she had chosen to come to us and not to some other convent. So far as this world is concerned Bernadette Soubirous no longer exists. We have taken into our care a child, Marie-Bernard, and it is our simple duty to treat her as we would any other novice—without regard for what may have happened in her past.

Marie-Thérèse. With all respect, Reverend Mother, that is not possible. No child can believe she has spoken to the Blessed Mother of God and not be proud. Only by remembering the cause can we cure the ill.

Rev. Mother. I know she must be protected at all costs against the sin of pride, and I know Marie-Bernard is no different in our eyes from any other novice, but this house will always be different in the world's eyes because she chose to come here.

Marie-Thérèse (*moving away down* R; *emphatically*) We should never have accepted her.

Rev. Mother. You think she has no vocation?

Marie-Thérèse. I think we allowed ourselves to be jostled. She had put herself in an impossible position. If she needed a retreat from the world . . . (*She breaks off*)

Rev. Mother. Mother Marie-Thérèse (*she rises; picks up the letter and turns to her*)—may I speak frankly?

Marie-Thérèse (*looking at her with surprise; bowing slightly*) It is my duty to listen to you at all times, Reverend Mother.

Rev. Mother (*taking a step towards her*) Duty can be a fine thing; but we should not always listen to each other for duty's sake. You must not be too critical of Sister Marie-Bernard. Her visions were not of her choosing. (*Turning down stage*) And she is far from strong—in fact her health has given me—and no doubt yourself—much cause for worry. It is for us to make her as good a nun as possible. But we must not drive her too hard. You find her apt?

Marie-Thérèse. Apt? I don't think apt is the word I would have chosen. She says her rosary continuously, yes. But aptitude for meditation—I can see none. No, nor any particular holiness, nor any deep reverence. In fact at times I find her positively pert.

Rev. Mother (*crossing below the table, down* L; *thinking it out as she speaks*) You complain of Sister Marie-Bernard for her pertness; I see it as a manifestation of high spirits. You complain she is lacking in reverence and true holiness; I see her as an unhappy child who has been singularly favoured, and is too simple to understand. Marie-Bernard may not yet have reached that high degree of sanctity achieved by so many men and women in the service of Our Lord, but we must never fall into the trap of saying, "Why her? Why not—one of them?"

MARIE-THÉRÈSE (*after a moment's wrestling with herself*) God knows I have prayed. I have prayed and prayed, Reverend Mother, not to think like that. I have lashed my soul with mortifications, I have examined my conscience well—but still I cannot believe. I say to myself every time I see her: Those eyes of yours have looked upon Our Lady; have glimpsed Heaven itself. I tell myself the Church recognizes this, that the evidence is beyond dispute and my reason must accept it. I have tried, Reverend Mother, God knows I have tried; but in my heart I cannot believe.

REV. MOTHER. And I, having looked into her eyes, cannot understand disbelief.

MARIE-THÉRÈSE. I want to believe. She has been here only six months and already I am exhausted. And there are years ahead . . .

REV. MOTHER. God willing, yes. I know how strong you are, and your great capacity for self-discipline—but there are times, when we can look too deeply into ourselves.

MARIE-THÉRÈSE. I will pray. I will pray God will help me to accept His choice.

(*A confused sound of young novices has been growing outside, and now* MARIE-VERONIQUE *and* MARIE-HEDWIGE *burst into the room from* L)

VERONIQUE (*coming* LC) I think it's silly . . . (*She sees Marie-Thérèse and breaks off in embarrassment; then she sees the Reverend Mother. She curtsies to each in turn*)

(MARIE-HEDWIGE *follows Marie-Veronique and stands* L *of her. She is equally abashed, and curtsies too*)

REV. MOTHER (*to Marie-Thérèse*) You may compliment Sister Marie-Emanuel on the way the medicine cupboard is kept.

(*The* REVEREND MOTHER *goes out* L, *leaving the door open*)

MARIE-THÉRÈSE (*moving above the* R *end of the table and indicating the linen*) If you are without occupation there is some linen here that needs mending. You can take it to the recreation room.

HEDWIGE. Yes, Mother.

MARIE-THÉRÈSE. And perhaps you would care to explain, Sister Marie-Veronique, what you consider silly?

Veronique. Silly, Mother? I don't know ...

Marie-Thérèse. As you entered this room I heard you say, "I think it's silly." What did you think was silly?

Hedwige. It was my fault, Mother.

Marie-Thérèse (*not unkindly*) I'm not blaming anyone, Sister. I asked a question—well?

Veronique. We were talking of the fuss the novices make when a new postulant arrives. It makes the girl feel so foolish.

Marie-Thérèse (*crossing below the table to* l; *tolerantly*) One day perhaps you'll learn that nothing we do here is without good reason. (*She moves* l *to the door, and turns*) There's a time for folly, you know. Even for being silly—when one is young.

(Marie-Thérèse *goes out* l)

Hedwige (*looking after her*) What could she mean by that?

Veronique. I've no idea. (*She moves in to the* l *end of the table and starts to sort the linen*)

Hedwige. I feel rather sorry for her.

Veronique. Sorry? For her? I should have thought she was the last person ...

Hedwige (*crossing up stage and down to the table*) Everyone dislikes her—just for doing her job. And yet she's not so bad. She can be quite human sometimes. Come to think of it, she must have been young once.

Veronique. And foolish?

Hedwige. Perhaps. Do you think she's "paying for it" now?

Veronique. Making us pay for it more likely. Oh, she's all right really. She doesn't mean any harm.

Hedwige. Not to us, perhaps. But there's one here ...

Veronique. Who?

Hedwige (*significantly*) I wouldn't be in her shoes for anything.

Veronique (*all attention*) You mean ... ?

Hedwige (*seriously*) It's not good to be Marie-Bernard.

Veronique (*enjoying the gossip*) You don't mean she hates her?

Hedwige (*quickly*) No, no. I'm sure she wouldn't be petty like that. (*Thinking it out*) She's severe only because it's good for us. But ...

Veronique. But what?

Hedwige (*unable to explain it*) I don't know. There's something ...

(Bernadette *enters* r. Marie-Veronique *sees her and changes the subject rather too brightly*)

Veronique (*fingering the mending*) It would be nice to make something that wasn't black or white.

Hedwige (*slow to follow the change*) Would it?

Veronique. Of course it would. Oh, you're just pretending. You don't really mean it.

BERNADETTE (*coming to* R *of Marie Hedwige*) Is that some mending to be done? May I help?

HEDWIGE. Mother Marie-Thérèse wants us to take it to the recreation room.

VERONIQUE. You can't lose all your love of pretty things just like that.

BERNADETTE. Just like what?

VERONIQUE. Poof! Presto! Just because we're inside these walls instead of outside. We're the same people we always were.

HEDWIGE. I wonder. You can't stay the same person after being cut off from the world even for eight months.

VERONIQUE. Look. Here's a veil. (*She holds it up*) Imagine, if we were allowed to embroider them, how the colours would glow.

HEDWIGE (*taking it from her and showing a long tear in the veil*) And how do you suppose a sedate nun could make a tear like that?

VERONIQUE. Not by climbing a tree.

BERNADETTE (*taking the veil from Marie-Hedwige, and moving* R *of the table*) It's too fine to darn neatly, and the black's so hard to see. (*She throws the veil over her novice's cap and tries to catch her reflection on the polished top of the table*) I wouldn't mind if it were mine to wear. (*There is no vanity here, only a tremendous longing to be a fully clothed nun and to have done with the period of waiting*)

(MARIE-THÉRÈSE *enters* L)

MARIE-THÉRÈSE. Sister Marie-Bernard!

(*For a moment* MARIE-THÉRÈSE *and* BERNADETTE *stand looking at each other. Then* BERNADETTE *realizes the other is referring to the veil, and she removes it*)

Such levity is out of place.

BERNADETTE (*simply; with the voice of obedience*) I am very sorry for my behaviour, and for my lack of industry. I did not mean to mock at my vocation.

MARIE-THÉRÈSE (*quietly*) I believe you. But you must know the importance of a good example to others. And I am afraid your action was not without vanity.

BERNADETTE. Oh, no.

MARIE-THÉRÈSE Oh, yes. (*She crosses above the table to* R *of it*)

(MARIE-VERONIQUE *and* MARIE-HEDWIGE *back up stage to make room for her*)

The table top was polished as an act of cleanliness, and for no other purpose. You are laying up Purgatory for yourself, Sister Marie-Bernard, years of Purgatory.

BERNADETTE. Yes, Mother.

MARIE-THÉRÈSE (*turning to the others*) You are all no doubt aware that a new postulant will be joining us today.

(MARIE-VERONIQUE *and* MARIE-HEDWIGE *come down to the* L *end of the table*)

I hope I can trust you to make her welcome. Her name will be Marie-Raphael and she has come to us from Rouen. She is leaving the shelter of a large and very devoted family. Be gentle with her. At the end of a few weeks, when she has become absorbed into our community, and her feet have been set on the path of self-abnegation, she will no doubt begin to count the world well lost. Work, my children, work hard that you may be lost in the community and found to God. Care nothing for outward show and obvious works of piety, for it is your soul God sees and will ultimately judge. Sister Marie-Bernard, go down to the kitchen and occupy yourself with the potatoes you will find there.

BERNADETTE. I have already prepared all the potatoes for tomorrow, Mother.

MARIE-THÉRÈSE (*with rising irritation*) The carrots then. You can scrub them for today's dinner.

BERNADETTE. If I do any more carrots, Mother, they will be wasted. I have already skinned as many as we can eat at one meal. (*She glances at her soiled hands, as though in confirmation*)

MARIE-THÉRÈSE (*determined to have the last word*) Then go into the Infirmary and tell Sister Marie-Emanuel I have sent you to polish furniture.

(BERNADETTE *turns to the door* R)

And, Sister Marie-Bernard . . .

BERNADETTE (*turning*) Yes, Mother?

MARIE-THÉRÈSE. I know your hands are soiled; but there is no disgrace in the marks of honest work.

BERNADETTE (*describing a circle in the air*) Whoever is without vanity let him put his finger through this circle.

(BERNADETTE *exits* R)

MARIE-THÉRÈSE (*after a momentary loss for words; turning to the others*) I must remind you again of the vow of obedience which requires your submission to the will of your superiors. It is their will that no mention of the visions of Lourdes, or of Sister Marie-Bernard's part in them shall be made either to her, or among yourselves in her absence.

(*There is a knock at the door* L)

Come in.

(MARIE-RAPHAEL *enters* L. *She is very timid and stands just inside the door*)

(*Looking at Marie-Raphael*) Ah, yes. (*To the others*) I told you some time ago to take your work to the recreation room. You had better hurry.

(Marie-Veronique *and* Marie-Hedwige *gather up the linen without enthusiasm, their thoughts and eyes on the newcomer*)

Marie-Thérèse (*moving below the* R *corner of the table*) Now, my child, come here.

(Marie-Raphael *crosses to her*)

There's no need to be frightened, we're not ogresses.

Raphael. I'm not frightened, really.

Marie-Thérèse. Just rather overwhelmed? Well, we shall see. You understand your name here will be Marie-Raphael? For here we leave behind all family ties.

Raphael. I understand.

Marie-Thérèse. The Reverend Mother will be here directly. (*To the Novices*) You had better hurry. (*To Marie-Raphael*) Afterwards you will meet your new companions. Can you sew?

Raphael. I'm not very clever at it. But I expect I shall improve with practice.

Marie-Thérèse. Then we must give you plenty of opportunity.

(*As* Marie-Hedwige *and* Marie-Veronique *are about to exit, the* Reverend Mother *enters* L, *and they stand aside for her. She crosses to the table and sits in the chair above it.* Marie-Hedwige *and* Marie-Veronique *exit, closing the door*)

This is Marie-Raphael, Reverend Mother, from Rouen.

Rev. Mother. Sit down, my child. (*She indicates the chair* R *of the table*)

(Marie-Raphael *sits.* Marie-Thérèse *moves behind her and stands* R *of the Reverend Mother*)

When I interviewed you before—let me see, that was two or three months ago?

Raphael. Two, Reverend Mother.

Rev. Mother. Yes. When I saw you two months ago I thought I could see the signs of a real vocation. I may have been wrong, of course, only time can test the truth of your calling, but I was sufficiently confident to admit you here.

Raphael. Thank you, Reverend Mother.

Rev. Mother. I think you told me you originally thought of entering the St Martory community? Why did you change your mind?

(Marie-Raphael *is silent*)

Rev. Mother. Come, child, you must surely know the reason?

Was it because you felt you could not be really happy in a contemplative order?

RAPHAEL. Yes.

REV. MOTHER. And yet you felt yourself drawn first of all to the spirit of Carmel. There are many communities that lead active lives and yet are closer to that spirit than we are here. Why did you not choose one of them?

RAPHAEL (*faltering*) I don't know. I don't think I can explain.

REV. MOTHER. Why not try? You'll find us very understanding.

(MARIE-RAPHAEL *is silent*)

Ah well! (*Changing the subject*) For the time being I will not bother you with a long list of regulations. Today you may spend the time getting used to us. Tomorrow you will join the novices' timetable. Is that clear?

RAPHAEL. Yes. Reverend Mother. (*She is about to rise*)

REV. MOTHER. Before you join the others you must know there is one subject we never mention within these walls. I refer to the events which took place in Lourdes eight years ago. Everyone is under obedience not to discuss them. You will be expected to conform. Is that understood?

RAPHAEL. Am I not to see her, then?

MARIE-THÉRÈSE. See whom, Mademoiselle? (*She moves R of Marie-Raphael*)

RAPHAEL. Bernadette.

MARIE-THÉRÈSE (*pouncing*) So you knew she was here?

RAPHAEL. Oh, yes.

REV. MOTHER. You seem to have gone to a great deal of trouble.

RAPHAEL. Everyone knows she has taken refuge here.

REV. MOTHER. Then everyone is misinformed, Mademoiselle. The person of whom you speak has not "taken refuge". She is here of her own free will to try her vocation with our community. Am I not right in thinking your enthusiasm for our convent was not untinged with enthusiasm for Bernadette?

(MARIE-RAPHAEL *hangs her head*)

I see that I am. My dear child, you might have spared yourself the trouble of thinking us such fools.

RAPHAEL. I'm sorry, Reverend Mother.

REV. MOTHER. Never mind.

RAPHAEL. I was afraid you might doubt my vocation if . . .

MARIE-THÉRÈSE. We are more likely to doubt your vocation if you lie to us.

RAPHAEL. Yes. (*To the Reverend Mother*) But I do want a religious life, truly, and ever since Bernadette touched my rosary

I've known that I could make a success of it—especially here with the saint herself.

(MARIE-THÉRÈSE *is about to speak but the* REVEREND MOTHER *stops her with a look*)

REV. MOTHER. You have a long way to go, Mademoiselle. You must never let me hear you make such a remark again. She is no saint. She has still to achieve her salvation. Did I understand you to say your rosary had been touched by her?

RAPHAEL. Yes; it was that . . .

REV. MOTHER. The one you have with you now?

RAPHAEL (*finding it in her reticule*) I carry it always. My aunt took me to the Grotto once—during one of her visions. I shall never forget it. And afterwards she passed quite close to me. I held out my rosary—and she touched it. Ever since then . . . (*She displays it with pride*)

REV. MOTHER. I think you have a vivid imagination. We must harness it to some useful purpose. Now, Mademoiselle, I must ask you, first of all, to promise me never to mention Lourdes or the visions or anything connected with them to anyone in this convent.

RAPHAEL. But . . .

REV. MOTHER. I must have your promise.

RAPHAEL. I promise.

REV. MOTHER. And now I want you to give me your rosary.

(*In silence* MARIE-RAPHAEL *hands her the rosary*)

Thank you. (*She crosses herself with the Crucifix on the rosary*) If you are to become a good religious your experiences must come to you at first hand. You are probably tired now; I will send somebody to show you your place. (*She rises*)

(MARIE-THÉRÈSE *crosses above the Reverend Mother to the door* L. MARIE-RAPHAEL *rises. The* REVEREND MOTHER *starts towards the door* L)

RAPHAEL. My rosary—am I not to have it back?

REV. MOTHER (*turning to her*) I will see that you have another to take its place. (*To Marie-Thérèse*) This will be given to some poor child whose parents cannot afford one. (*She hands the rosary to her*)

(MARIE-THÉRÈSE *goes out* L)

(*Very gently*) You cannot win a place in Heaven through the graces of another. You have made a good beginning and have learnt well your first lesson in obedience.

(*The* REVEREND MOTHER *exits* L. MARIE-RAPHAEL *stands for a moment looking sadly after her. Then she drops back into her chair, and the tears come.*

BERNADETTE *enters* R. *She takes in the situation at a glance and at once becomes very practical)*

BERNADETTE *(shutting the door)* I cried, too, on my first day.

(MARIE-RAPHAEL *rises, fumbling for her handkerchief and turns away below the table)*

All day and quite a way into the night. The Sisters told me it's a sign of a true vocation. *(She moves to the chair* R *of the table)*

RAPHAEL. It's stupid of me, I know. I wanted to come. And now . . . I didn't think it would be so difficult. *(She looks round the room seeking something)*

BERNADETTE. You won't find a mirror here. You'll just have to mop your eyes and hope for the best. I was sent to polish furniture as a punishment for looking at myself in the table top. Now it's all so clean, and I got so out of breath, Sister Marie-Emanuel told me to stop. *(She sinks into the chair)*

RAPHAEL *(turning to her)* What's your name?

BERNADETTE. Marie-Bernard. You're Marie-Raphael, aren't you?

RAPHAEL. How did you know?

BERNADETTE. We were told you were coming. How could we make you welcome if we didn't know your name?

RAPHAEL. I've seen you before. Did you live in Rouen before —before you came here?

BERNADETTE. No. Never.

RAPHAEL. I'm sure . . .

BERNADETTE *(rising)* You mustn't be too sure. We all look very much alike with these caps. It's the hair that makes us different, you know. And the Sisters are even worse with their veils. *(She rises)* You'll find the only way to recognize some of them is from behind—by the way they walk. *(She illustrates her words with a little walk down* R *and back)*

(MARIE-RAPHAEL *laughs and moves below the table)*

That's better. *(She crosses to Marie-Raphael)* You're going to like it here, and we're all going to like you. I can see that.

RAPHAEL. Do we have to work very hard?

BERNADETTE. It's good to be well occupied. It makes the days seem shorter. We do our fair share. *(She crosses and moves up* L*)* And there is more peace here than I have ever known outside. *(Turning)* We're loved and protected—but sometimes one feels so tired.

RAPHAEL. I'm sorry . . .

BERNADETTE. Oh, you mustn't mind me. For you there'll be plenty of laughter and fun, for there's a time to play as well as to work in this family.

RAPHAEL *(her hands going in search of her rosary; with a nervous laugh*) Silly of me; I keep feeling for my rosary and it isn't here.

BERNADETTE (*concerned*) Why, have you lost it?

RAPHAEL. Reverend Mother took it away. She said she'd give me another.

BERNADETTE (*coming down to her*) Was it very precious?

RAPHAEL. I'd promised myself I'd never part with it. It was quite ordinary, but . . .

BERNADETTE. One rosary's as good as another. It's the prayers that count.

(MARIE-THÉRÈSE *enters* L. *She has a new rosary in her hand*)

MARIE-THÉRÈSE (*standing by the door; slightly put out*) I see Sister Marie-Bernard has been looking after you. If you will go through this door you will find Sister Marie-Veronique. She will take you down to the refectory and give you a hot drink. I hope you will quickly come to look upon this as your home. We shall regard you as our daughter.

(MARIE-RAPHAEL *starts towards the door*)

One moment. The Reverend Mother asked me to give you this. (*She holds out the rosary, and takes a step forward*)

(MARIE-RAPHAEL *takes the rosary, but in her nervousness drops it.* BERNADETTE *steps forward between them, picks it up and gives it to the girl*)

RAPHAEL. Thank you.

MARIE-THÉRÈSE (*crossing below the table; suppressing her anger*) Sister Marie-Bernard, you will remain. (*Turning to Marie-Raphael*) You may go now.

(*And with a shy smile at Bernadette* MARIE-RAPHAEL *goes out* L)

Sister Marie-Bernard, permission has been granted for you to meet a Franciscan father who is visiting Nevers.

(BERNADETTE *closes the door*)

He is here now, and you will be sent for when he is ready to receive you. Until then you may spend the time recapturing the memories of your life in Lourdes.

BERNADETTE. I don't need any time to remember them.

MARIE-THÉRÈSE (*moving up* R) He will wish to question you and any discrepancies in your story will look bad.

BERNADETTE. Whatever he asks me I will tell him—with the Reverend Mother's permission, of course.

MARIE-THÉRÈSE (*turning to her*) Of course. For this occasion you have permission. But at no other time. Is that clear?

BERNADETTE (*moving a few steps to* LC) I have never spoken of that life, except under obedience, since I came here.

MARIE-THÉRÈSE. Are you quite sure?

BERNADETTE. I know how to hold my tongue.

MARIE-THÉRÈSE (*coming down below the chair* R *of the table*) And I know what chatterboxes you peasant girls can be.

BERNADETTE. I have never lied to you. Because we were poor and mother took in washing, it doesn't mean we were brought up to lie and cheat. Mother has always been as strict as you are . . .

MARIE-THÉRÈSE. I seem to remember your father was in prison once. (*She sits* R *of the table*)

BERNADETTE. There is no shame in that. The poor are often in prison. I'm proud of my father; and my mother never let us go dirty or untidy if she could help it.

MARIE-THÉRÈSE. Pride, Sister, pride . . .

BERNADETTE. God tells us to honour our father and mother; there cannot be sin in that.

MARIE-THÉRÈSE. And did your Lady tell you to defy authority?

BERNADETTE. Must you remind me! I shall never see Lourdes again nor my Lady, until I die. (*She sits* L *of the table*) It's so lonely. I know I must speak of these things under obedience, but not now. Please not now. Please, please let me keep them to myself.

MARIE-THÉRÈSE. The privilege you were granted was a very great one. It cannot have been meant for you alone. Your Lady would not want you to keep those wonderful secrets to yourself if they could help others. She would not wish you to be selfish.

BERNADETTE (*wearily; this is not the first time the conversation has taken this trend*) She told me what I was to keep to myself and what I was to tell others. I have told you everything I am allowed.

MARIE-THÉRÈSE. Have you? Are you quite sure? Think how dreadful it would be if your memory were to play you false.

BERNADETTE. My Lady would not allow me to forget anything.

MARIE-THÉRÈSE (*rising*) Do you think the Mother of God has nothing better to do than jog your memory for you?

BERNADETTE (*obstinately*) I know my Lady would never break a promise. And I shall never tell the secrets she gave to me.

MARIE-THÉRÈSE. No, I don't think you will. (*She looks at Bernadette long and searchingly*) Are they to die with you?

(BERNADETTE *is silent*)

(*As she speaks she moves round above the table to* L *of Bernadette*) If you were given some special knowledge I should have thought it would have been your duty to keep it in this world. (*She is tempting her to speak*)

(BERNADETTE *is still silent*)

(*Becoming exasperated*) When I think of the things you are supposed to have been told, and the little you have done, I tremble for the fate of your soul.

BERNADETTE. I don't know why my Lady chose me, but she did. And she knows I have done all she asked of me. Now I have only to suffer, and pray for sinners.

MARIE-THÉRÈSE. Take care, child, take care.

BERNADETTE. With your help, Mother, I will try to be worthy of my Lady.

(*For a moment* MARIE-THÉRÈSE *looks deeply into Bernadette's face*)

MARIE-THÉRÈSE (*almost to herself*) Those eyes . . . Those eyes . . . O God . . . Pride, my daughter; pride; let there be no place for it in your soul. Cast it out.

BERNADETTE (*in a whisper*) Yes, Mother.

MARIE-THÉRÈSE. You must be proud, you must. You who have . . . (*She crosses above the table to* RC; *her voice hardens*) You have touched rosaries and given the trimmings of your hair for keepsakes . . . (*Turning*) If you are not proud why did you do these things? Why?

BERNADETTE. It made people happy.

MARIE-THÉRÈSE. And do you still do it?

BERNADETTE. No. It meant nothing.

MARIE-THÉRÈSE (*moving in to* R *of the table*) Are you sure? Are you quite sure?

BERNADETTE. I have been forbidden.

MARIE-THÉRÈSE (*crossing below the table to* L) You might do it for a novice, if it means nothing.

BERNADETTE. They never speak of Lourdes.

MARIE-THÉRÈSE (*turning*) How do you know? Do you know more about them than I do? (*Looking at the door* L) There's one of them here now might ask you to bless her new rosary . . .

BERNADETTE. I wouldn't do anything so blasphemous. I have never blessed a rosary.

MARIE-THÉRÈSE (*closing in to her*) When you touched them, what were you doing then?

BERNADETTE. I have told you, Mother, I only did it to give a friend a present—a remembrance; I hoped they would pray for me.

MARIE-THÉRÈSE (*moving behind her*) And what sort of present was your touch? And what about your hair?

BERNADETTE. Please! (*She rises*) You make my head go round and round as if you were trying to trap me.

MARIE-THÉRÈSE (*turning above the table*) If you can think that of your Novice Mistress it only goes to show how far you have to travel. (*She sits above the table*)

BERNADETTE. Yes, Mother.

(*For the moment it seems there is nothing more to be said*)

Marie-Thérèse (*holding out the rosary*) Do you recognize this?

Bernadette (*turning and breaking away a little*) No.

Marie-Thérèse. You have never seen it before? You are sure? Look closely at it.

(Bernadette *steps forward to look at it*)

It means nothing to you?

Bernadette. Why should it?

Marie-Thérèse. Because it belonged to Marie-Raphael.

Bernadette. The one that Reverend Mother took away from her?

Marie-Thérèse. So you knew that?

Bernadette. She told me. It made her cry.

Marie-Thérèse. And why should it make her cry? What is so special about this rosary?

Bernadette. I don't know. Did her mother give it to her? Or perhaps she had it for her First Communion.

Marie-Thérèse. You know that was not the reason. You know very well why she was so distressed at parting with it. Because you had touched it.

Bernadette. Oh, no! (*She backs away up* L) But I touched so many. I didn't know. Please may she have it back. Please! If I had known it could ever make her unhappy . . .

Marie-Thérèse. You see now the harm you have done? No, she will not have it back. (*She puts it away inside her habit*) Such relics of hysteria and exhibitionism have no place in a convent.

Bernadette (*coming down* LC) When first I came here I felt happiness and peace all around, warming me like sunshine. I thought . . . I thought . . . (*But she cannot voice her thought*) How hard life can be, even in the sun.

Marie-Thérèse. All life is hard. From birth to death for everyone it's a battlefield. (*She rises and comes down to* R *of Bernadette*) But some of us have been chosen by God to fight for the souls of others as well as for our own. I have fought for you, Sister Marie-Bernard, and I will continue to fight, that in the end you may be won for God.

Bernadette (*turning to her*) Fight for me, Mother, yes, if you must, but pray for me, too. I have great need of prayers—your prayers.

Marie-Thérèse. Whatever the Lady of your visions—if they were visions—promised, Heaven is not in your pocket.

Bernadette (*turning away*) She never promised me Heaven. And I know I shall not go there unless I pray and suffer well in this life. (*Turning to her*) But they were real, the visions, I know they were. I know it. I know it . . .

Marie-Thérèse (*facing her*) If you are so sure, why must you keep telling yourself so?

BERNADETTE. I am sure. I am. It is you I am telling. You are the one who is not sure.

(*For a moment* MARIE-THÉRÈSE *stares at Bernadette unable to answer the truth of this. Then from a distant part of the convent there is the sound of a bell*)

MARIE-THÉRÈSE (*moving away to* RC) Should the Father ask you, you are sure you remember exactly what the Lady looked like?

BERNADETTE. I shall never forget her as long as I live.

MARIE-THÉRÈSE (*turning to her*) Memories can fade with time.

BERNADETTE. This one will be with me till I die. And when I die I'll have no need of it for then I'll be with her. (*She moves towards Marie-Thérèse below the table*) Oh, Mother, pray for me. Pray. God's will be done and I know I must suffer, as He suffered; and it's a sin to wish for rest before He wills it; but there are times—times when I hear of death—and my heart is filled with envy.

MARIE-THÉRÈSE. Self, self, self! Have you no pity for the dead?

BERNADETTE. Pity? Of course I've pity. And I'm very sad for them, and for those they have left behind. Although it seems strange we should feel sad for those who have gone to Heaven.

MARIE-THÉRÈSE. Then it may comfort you to know that your mother is now at peace in God. We had news of her death today.

BERNADETTE. My mother!

MARIE-THÉRÈSE. For her the struggle is over.

(*The* REVEREND MOTHER *enters. She appreciates the situation at once*)

She had a hard life. Now she is at rest.

(BERNADETTE *stands in silence. The* REVEREND MOTHER *crosses to* L *of her and lays a hand on her shoulder*)

REV. MOTHER. You were very fond of her, I think. Very close to her. You don't have to stop loving her now, you know. You can still pray for each other.

(*There is a moment's silence*)

You will find our guest in the parlour. You have permission to answer any questions he may put to you.

(BERNADETTE *turns to go. A sob breaks from her. The* REVEREND MOTHER *looks at* MARIE-THÉRÈSE, *who turns away.*
The REVEREND MOTHER *follows* BERNADETTE *off. As the door shuts behind them* MARIE-THÉRÈSE *drops into an attitude of prayer. But the words will not come and slowly her eyes fill with tears*)

Marie-Thérèse. I cannot even pray. Teach me to be sure. Show me.

(*The* Lights *fade to blackness, and the* Curtain *falls.*

When the Curtain *rises, and the* Lights *come up, the room is empty·* Marie-Veronique *comes quickly and gaily into the room from* L. *She is carrying a box of medical supplies.* Marie-Hedwige *follows close behind*)

Hedwige. Really, Sister Marie-Veronique, you shouldn't do things like that. The poor girl was most unhappy.

Veronique (*crossing above the table*) Nonsense, she loved it. Every minute of it. But I'll make it up to her. (*She puts the box on the table*) What shall we do with these?

Hedwige (*taking the lid off*) Are you never afraid of being found out? One day Reverend Mother really will be there.

Veronique. One day she was. (*She starts to unpack, handing the small packages to Marie-Hedwige*)

Hedwige. No!

Veronique. It was wonderful. Let's put these in the cupboard. I was never so frightened since I slid down the little glacier at Gavarnie.

Hedwige. But what happened? (*She is taking packages to the cupboard all the time*)

Veronique. Nothing.

Hedwige. Nothing? Wasn't she terribly angry?

Veronique. She never knew.

Hedwige. You don't mean you lied to her?

Veronique. Of course not. Is there room for another? I'd always tell the truth, however scared I was, if I had to. But we didn't. At least not all of it.

Hedwige (*back at the table*) If I hadn't known you for the last twelve years I'd say you didn't belong in this place.

Veronique. I belong here all right. (*Finding something in the box*) Oh!

Hedwige. What's the matter?

Veronique. Here's a list. Should we be checking them, do you think?

Hedwige. Sister Marie-Raphael's not likely to thank us if there's anything missing.

Veronique (*crossing to the cupboard*) We can't take them all out again. Must we? There never is.

Hedwige. Still the same, Sister Marie-Veronique. Will nothing change you?

Veronique (*cheerfully*) Nothing. Poor Sister Marie-Hedwige, what a trial I am to you.

(*Her laughter is infectious and* Marie-Hedwige *joins in*)

Hedwige. You're quite incorrigible.

(*In the midst of their laughter comes* MARIE-RAPHAEL *from the Infirmary*)

RAPHAEL (*standing by the door* R) Sisters! Sisters! What a noise to make outside a sick-room door.

VERONIQUE (*stricken*) We haven't woken one of your patients, have we? (*Coming to* L *of the table*) It was all my fault. I was daring Sister Marie-Hedwige to forget her solemnity. Are we forgiven? Please, Sister Marie-Raphael?

RAPHAEL (*moving to the chair* R *of the table*) I can forgive you easily enough. And I'm sure Sister Marie-Bernard will, too. She likes your joyful noise—at least she says she does . . . (*She sits wearily*)

(MARIE-HEDWIGE *crosses* R *above the table*)

VERONIQUE. Well, then . . .

RAPHAEL. But it's not good for her. Most nights she has no sleep.

HEDWIGE (*coming to* R *of Marie-Raphael; compassionately*) And nor do you.

RAPHAEL (*quietly*) No.

HEDWIGE. You should spare yourself a little. Let me do something. I'll ask . . .

RAPHAEL (*almost fiercely*) It's my job. Besides . . .

HEDWIGE. Besides what?

RAPHAEL. I understand her asthma. I know how to make her comfortable. I must go back . . . (*She tries to rise*)

HEDWIGE (*stopping her*) You'll make yourself ill.

RAPHAEL. Let me go. She's sitting up today.

VERONIQUE. She's better then?

HEDWIGE. I know about asthma. I helped to nurse my father once. I'll get permission . . .

RAPHAEL (*almost desperately*) It's not only her asthma . . .

HEDWIGE. There's something else?

VERONIQUE. She isn't really ill again? She isn't going to die this time, is she?

RAPHAEL (*after a pause; with determination*) No. Let me go back, please.

HEDWIGE (*firmly*) What else? You haven't told us yet.

RAPHAEL. It's her leg, I think. I don't know. Only Reverend Mother really knows.

VERONIQUE. But her leg's been bad for months . . .

RAPHAEL. Well, now it's worse. Worse than it's ever been. It's very painful. She's often in great agony. And she tries so hard not to cry out—she thinks she will disturb us. As if she ever could.

(BERNADETTE *enters from the Infirmary. She now walks with great difficulty owing to the pain in her right leg. But although she is obviously a very sick woman she does everything to minimize it*)

(*Seeing Bernadette, rising and hurrying to her*) Now what are you doing here? You should be in your chair.

BERNADETTE. Let me stay. It's high time I was about again and doing some work. I'm becoming a real lazybones.

(MARIE-RAPHAEL *leads her to the chair* R *of the table*)

HEDWIGE. Of course you're not.

RAPHAEL. You shouldn't have left the Infirmary. You're very naughty.

BERNADETTE. I can as well sit in a chair and work here, as sit in there. I'm much better today. Much better.

RAPHAEL. Nevertheless . . .

BERNADETTE. Don't scold me, please. You should know it's bad for your patients to scold them. Now I've finished the doves, and I must find some more work.

VERONIQUE. Have you been making the doves for the May altar? Do let us see them?

BERNADETTE. Of course. (*And she is about to go into the Infirmary to fetch them*)

RAPHAEL. You stay here. I'll fetch them.

BERNADETTE. They're very frail . . .

RAPHAEL. I can take care of them . . .

(MARIE-RAPHAEL *exits* R)

BERNADETTE. I'm a fine one to talk. I spoilt four of them myself with my clumsy fingers. We must find something to pack them away in.

HEDWIGE (*setting the chair* R *of the table*) Sit down here and rest yourself. Would you like me to get you a pillow for your back?

BERNADETTE (*sitting*) You mustn't fuss me. I've told you I'm much better.

HEDWIGE. But your leg, Sister? (*She stands* R *of Bernadette*)

BERNADETTE. My leg is well enough. In any case it will have to do as it's told like the rest of us.

VERONIQUE (*crossing above the table to* L *of Bernadette*) You should take more care of yourself.

BERNADETTE (*gently chiding*) I am in God's hands.

(MARIE-RAPHAEL *enters with the six paper doves in her hands*)

RAPHAEL (*crossing above Bernadette*) Help me to put these down.

(MARIE-VERONIQUE *and* MARIE-HEDWIGE *move to the* L *end above the table*)

HEDWIGE (*taking them one by one out of her hands*) They can go in this box. (*And she packs them in the box they have just emptied on the table*)

VERONIQUE (*coming between Marie-Raphael and Marie-Hedwige*) They're beautiful. (*She picks one up*)

(MARIE-RAPHAEL, *having set down her burden crosses behind Bernadette to R of her*)

BERNADETTE (*holding out her hand for Marie-Veronique's dove*) He is my favourite. He's smaller than the rest. (*She raises the bird and allows it to touch against her cheek for an instant*)

VERONIQUE (*taking the bird from her, still full of admiration*) It must have taken you weeks to make them. (*She puts it in the box*)

BERNADETTE. Only one week. Is there some paper to cover them?

(MARIE-HEDWIGE *has already found a piece of tissue-paper in the box and she carefully lays it over the birds*)

VERONIQUE (*still a little overcome*) And to think the other day we were afraid we were going to lose you.

BERNADETTE (*purposely misunderstanding*) Lose me? I had not heard. None of the other houses would want an old crock like me.

HEDWIGE. Sister Marie-Veronique meant we were afraid you were going to die.

RAPHAEL. No! (*She moves in close to Bernadette*)

BERNADETTE (*her hand seeking Marie-Raphael's*) Then you were all afraid for nothing. God is in no hurry to have a useless thing like me cluttering up His heaven.

RAPHAEL. How can you speak like that? You're not useless. You're worth more than all of us put together. (*To the others*) Leave her, please. Can't you see . . .

BERNADETTE. Sister Marie-Raphael?

RAPHAEL. What is it?

BERNADETTE. What do you do with a broom?

RAPHAEL. With a broom? Why sweep the floor of course.

BERNADETTE. And when you have finished sweeping, what then?

RAPHAEL. You put it away. But . . .

BERNADETTE. Where?

RAPHAEL. In the corner behind the door.

BERNADETTE. Exactly.

VERONIQUE (*gently, after digesting this*) Never in this world, nor the next.

BERNADETTE. For twelve years now I have been behind the doors of this convent.

VERONIQUE. Now you are purposely misunderstanding me. We all know . . .

HEDWIGE (*to Marie-Veronique*) Hush, Sister, hush . . .

VERONIQUE. I won't be quiet. (*She passes Marie-Hedwige and moves swiftly round the L end of the table and below it*) Everybody knows what a source of inspiration Sister Marie-Bernard has been . . .

BERNADETTE (*rising*) Stop it, stop it! That's a stupid thing to say.

RAPHAEL. It's my fault. I should never have left you. Come
back to your chair . . .
BERNADETTE (*with a flash of her old temper*) You talk like fools.
Leave me alone, leave me, all of you.
VERONIQUE (*kneeling; in tears*) Forgive me, I didn't mean . . .
BERNADETTE (*really angry now*) Get up! Get up at once.

(MARIE-THÉRÈSE *appears in the doorway* L. *In her hands is a
bundle of clothes. There is a moment's appalled silence, then* MARIE-
VERONIQUE *scrambles to her feet.* MARIE-THÉRÈSE *moves in eloquent
silence above the table*)

MARIE-THÉRÈSE. We have been sent some old clothing to give
to the poor. It will need sorting—(*she dumps it on the paper covering
the doves*) and probably mending.

(*All the Nuns react, and* MARIE-VERONIQUE *almost cries out, but*
BERNADETTE *stops her*)

MARIE-THÉRÈSE. As it is obvious you have nothing better to
do you can make a start on it at once. (*To Marie-Veronique*) You
were about to say something?
BERNADETTE (*quickly*) May I be allowed to help, Mother? I
would like some more work to do.
MARIE-THÉRÈSE. More work? And what is the work you have
been doing? I thought you'd been lying in bed for at least a week.
BERNADETTE. Yes, Mother. But I've been learning.
MARIE-THÉRÈSE. Learning?
BERNADETTE. To be an invalid.
MARIE-THÉRÈSE. That should be easy enough for you. You've
had enough practice. I even seem to remember one night when
we had to rouse the Bishop so you might make your profession,
because you were in extremis.
BERNADETTE. Had I been able to speak I would have told you I
was not going to die.
MARIE-THÉRÈSE. No doubt. There's a name for that sort of
sickness.

(MARIE-RAPHAEL *can hardly control herself*)

BERNADETTE. Yes, Mother. I'll ask if I may go back to my
duties in the Sacristy.
RAPHAEL. But you're not fit to . . .
MARIE-THÉRÈSE. I think Sister Marie-Bernard can be left to
know best what she is fit to do. Sister Marie-Veronique, take that
pile of clothing elsewhere and deal with it. You may go, too,
Sister.

(MARIE-VERONIQUE *and* MARIE-HEDWIGE *exchange glances.
Then the former, somewhat flustered, gathers up the clothes, spilling
one or two pieces, and hurries out,* L. MARIE-HEDWIGE *about to go,
sees the remainder and collects them*)

HEDWIGE. Sister Marie-Veronique, you've forgotten half of them . . .

(MARIE-HEDWIGE *follows her out* L)

MARIE-THÉRÈSE (*to Bernadette*) What efforts have you ever made to overcome your weakness?

BERNADETTE. I have prayed.

MARIE-THÉRÈSE. The help of Heaven is not given except we help ourselves.

RAPHAEL. But, Mother, she has been in great pain.

BERNADETTE. Suffering pain, Sister, is far less painful than nursing it.

MARIE-THÉRÈSE (*to Marie-Raphael*) If you persist in expressing unwanted and irresponsible opinions you will have to give up your charge. (*To Bernadette*) Why have you never been to Lourdes We offered to take you there to try the healing waters for yourself. Have you no faith?

BERNADETTE. I was not told to go.

MARIE-THÉRÈSE. If you want to be cured you surely don't wait to be sent under obedience?

BERNADETTE. Those waters are not for me.

MARIE-THÉRÈSE. If they can cure others . . .

BERNADETTE. My Lady does not want me to go.

MARIE-THÉRÈSE (*moving away* L) Your Lady! Always your Lady! And very convenient she is, too. (*Turning*) I tell you there was no Lady. It was hysteria.

BERNADETTE (*in a whisper*) No, Mother.

MARIE-THÉRÈSE. Yes, Sister. There was no Lady. All these years you've fooled us, haven't you? The rose bush never flowered.

BERNADETTE. Of course not. Father Peyramale never hoped it would.

RAPHAEL. I wonder . . .

BERNADETTE. He was ashamed of asking.

RAPHAEL. Perhaps it was wrong to look for the roses among the thorns.

MARIE-THÉRÈSE (*dismissing it*) You talk in riddles.

RAPHAEL (*fingering her rosary*) All these years they have been in the hands of the suppliants, every bead a rose and every rose a prayer. (*Suddenly she moves to Bernadette and stands close beside her*)

(BERNADETTE, *who has been almost exhausted by the attack, seems to draw strength from Marie-Raphael's presence*)

MARIE-THÉRÈSE (*recovering herself*) If you want some work to do you can make a start on the doves for the May altar. You had better make nine of them and I will pick out the six best. Sister Marie-Raphael can collect the materials for you (*with significance*) —now.

BERNADETTE (*quickly, before Marie-Raphael can say anything*) You know what we need, Sister; plenty of white breast feathers—as many as you can find—and a few larger ones. I think we have enough paper, and there's cotton-wool up here.

(MARIE-RAPHAEL *hastens off* L)

MARIE-THÉRÈSE. When I entered the room it seemed to me I disturbed an emotional fracas.

BERNADETTE. I'm very sorry, Mother. (*She sits* R *of the table*)

MARIE-THÉRÈSE. I'm not asking for an apology . . .

BERNADETTE. Sister Marie-Veronique was upset.

MARIE-THÉRÈSE. That was obvious. (*She moves round to the front of the table*)

BERNADETTE. It was my fault. My wicked temper ran away with me again.

MARIE-THÉRÈSE. I see. I was mistaken. (*She moves to* L *of Bernadette*) I thought it was Sister Marie-Veronique on her knees begging your forgiveness.

BERNADETTE. She had tempted me to lose my temper, and she asked me to forgive her. But it was not her fault, Mother. I need very little temptation as you well know.

MARIE-THÉRÈSE. Indeed. (*She crosses Bernadette to* RC) Had it not been for your temper I might have found it easier to believe in you.

BERNADETTE (*sincerely*) That would have made me very happy, Mother.

MARIE-THÉRÈSE (*turning and looking at her; seeing her almost in a new light*) Yes. I believe it would. Poor child! You have had quite an affection for me, haven't you?

BERNADETTE. Almost as though you had been my real mother.

MARIE-THÉRÈSE. I have tried to be a mother to you in God. I have tried. Everything I have done has been for your good.

BERNADETTE. And that must be my comfort. (*Practically, with no hint of self-pity*) But it's a dull diet, Mother; like living on onion soup all one's life.

MARIE-THÉRÈSE. The path of humility is dull—and hard.

BERNADETTE. And I would not have it otherwise. My mother often scolded me as a child, but I knew it was necessary, and I knew there was always love in her heart.

MARIE-THÉRÈSE (*accepting the implication*) God help me, I've failed.

BERNADETTE. No, Mother.

MARIE-THÉRÈSE. For twelve years it has been my lot to strive for you, and now I know I've failed. It was my pride. Yes, I've had my pride to fight as well. When first I heard you were coming to us, I was proud to think you would be in my care; that I had been found fit to guide His chosen child, the honoured friend of His Holy Mother. I thought—just like all the others—I could

draw inspiration from her. I thought the eyes that had looked on
the Holy Mother of God herself would help me to see better.

(*A bell starts tolling*)

BERNADETTE. Instead you found an ignorant peasant girl, with
a sharp tongue, who was no ready-made saint. Poor Mother!
What have I done to you? (*Impulsively she takes her hand and raises it
to her lips*) Thank you for all your kindness.

(MARIE-THÉRÈSE *withdraws her hand, refusing to let the moment
overwhelm her*)

MARIE-THÉRÈSE. I must go down to the chapel. (*Crossing above
the table*) Perhaps you will be fit to follow today? (*Seeing the box
on the table*) Always leaving their rubbish about. Why can't these
Sisters be tidy? (*She picks up the box with the intention of taking it
away, and disturbs the paper. Realizing what is underneath it she gives
Bernadette a searching look, puts the box back on the table, and turns to go,
saying under her breath*) Hypocrite!

(MARIE-THÉRÈSE *exits* L.
    The bell continues to toll. BERNADETTE *rises from her chair and
starts to follow. But she is exhausted physically and mentally, and the
effort is too much for her pain-racked body. She sinks to the floor, just
able to turn towards the little statue of the Virgin Mary near the
Infirmary door*)

BERNADETTE (*unable even to make the Sign of the Cross*) Hail Mary,
full of grace, the Lord is with thee. Blessed art thou among women
and . . . Holy Mother, I knew the way would be hard, and even
painful, and I've never minded that—but must it be so lonely?
You know I would be in the chapel now if I could reach it, and
truly I've tried to be there, but—but my legs will not obey me
any longer. Please let this be my chapel for today—and tomorrow
—tomorrow I . . . Holy Mother, help me to keep my eyes on the
Cross.

(MARIE-RAPHAEL *appears in the doorway* L. *For a moment she
stands watching the praying girl, but unseen by her*)

—keep me faithful even unto death, and pray for me, a sinner,
now and at the hour of . . . Help me, please.

(MARIE-RAPHAEL *moves swiftly to Bernadette and raises her a
little.* BERNADETTE's *hands appear to be seeking something in the
folds of her habit*)

My rosary . . . a crucifix . . .

(MARIE-RAPHAEL *takes out her own rosary and holds it out to
Bernadette.*

The LIGHTS *fade to blackness, and the* CURTAIN *falls. Outside the*

minute bell begins its measured tolling. In the distance the voices
of the nuns can be heard chanting the Dies Irae. The singing dies
away.

The Curtain *rises, and the* Lights *come up. The* Reverend Mother
enters from the Infirmary. She is carrying in one hand a small lighted
lamp, and in the other a little exercise-book, partially open, that she has
been trying to read. Going to the table she puts down the lamp, sits r *of*
it, and becomes absorbed in the little book.

 Marie-Thérèse *enters* r *and crosses to the door* l)

Rev. Mother. Mother.

Marie-Thérèse. Yes, Reverend Mother. (*She waits expectantly*)

 (*The* Reverend Mother *continues to read in silence for a while,*
oblivious of the other's presence. Marie-Thérèse *makes an impatient*
movement)

Rev. Mother (*at last*) Have you seen this?

Marie-Thérèse. That exercise-book? Yes, I believe I have.
Whose is it?

Rev. Mother. It was Sister Marie-Bernard's. You didn't read
it, of course?

Marie-Thérèse. Why, is it of consequence?

Rev. Mother. Everything to do with Sister Marie-Bernard is
of consequence. Take it with you and read it. You'll learn a great
deal. (*She offers her the book*)

Marie-Thérèse (*moving in above the table; almost at the end of her*
tether) Must I learn more? I had hoped that now . . . Have I
discharged my duty well?

Rev. Mother. Only your conscience can answer that. Mean-
time this may help you. (*She holds out the book again*)

 (Marie-Thérèse *takes the book and is about to open it*)

Marie-Thérèse. Was I too hard on her?

Rev. Mother. Why do you ask me that—now?

Marie-Thérèse. I've heard them whispering behind their
hands; I've caught the looks they exchanged behind my back. . . .
I know what the novices thought . . .

Rev. Mother. When we accepted her we knew the responsibility. For her own good we had to crush the elements of pride.
And she knew it, too. It's there. She understood—and she forgave.
I am sure if it were not for the strain of these past weeks—and
indeed years—you would see the ridiculousness of your self-
reproaches.

Marie-Thérèse. So often a word of kindness would have
helped her through her day—and I withheld it. I must take my
share of blame.

Rev. Mother (*with growing irritation*) No-one is to blame. And
if you persist in living in the past, you will wreck yourself on rocks

far harder than a stony heart—the rocks of a little grotto in the foothills of the Pyrenees.

MARIE-THÉRÈSE. I hope and pray it may never be my fate to go to Lourdes again. The sight of pilgrims travelling with such faith—and all because of an ignorant peasant girl . . .

REV. MOTHER. Because of a peasant girl and God. (*Indicating the book*) There is the record of her—ignorance.

MARIE-THÉRÈSE. She was a mystic, and I never knew? Is that what you're trying to tell me?

REV. MOTHER. Read for yourself.

MARIE-THÉRÈSE. That little untutored mind could make a record of her path to sanctity? What are you asking me to believe?

REV. MOTHER. It's not for me to ask you to believe anything.

MARIE-THÉRÈSE. How much do you believe? Was she a saint?

REV. MOTHER. Only the future can decide that. I think she had qualities of saintliness.

MARIE-THÉRÈSE. Then I hope her cause is not promoted in my lifetime.

REV. MOTHER. Her cause?

MARIE-THÉRÈSE. I could not answer to her sanctity. The very thought is frightening to me. (*She moves to the chair* L *of the table*)

REV. MOTHER. You are a woman of great integrity. Whatever your private doubts, I know you would give a clear statement of the facts.

MARIE-THÉRÈSE (*sitting*) No, they will want more. They will say, after her confessor, I must know better than anyone the state of her soul. I tell you I don't. If she had opened her heart to me, if she had told me her secrets, I would have guided and counselled her. I would have brought all the years of my experience to the task. Together we could have created a wonderful experience of spiritual greatness. And now it is too late.

REV. MOTHER (*gently*) She has made her own greatness, Mother Marie-Thérèse, and she needed no help. She has followed the little path of insignificance, and has made of it something great and glorious. Her life has been a revelation, and the record of it will be her place in history. I have been thinking what inscription should be placed over her body. (*She takes a piece of paper from her habit*) In life she was without corruption; and now in death . . . She must, of course, have the same as any other member of our order who has died here. (*She reads from the paper*) "Bernadette Soubirous. In religion Sister Marie-Bernard. Departed this life in the Mother House of the Sisters of Charity at Nevers, on April sixteenth, eighteen seventy-nine, in the thirty-sixth year of her age and the twelfth year of her religious profession." (*Picking up a pen*) But perhaps there is something else we could add? Shall we say: (*writing*) "Favoured at Lourdes in the year eighteen fifty-eight by Visions of the Blessed Virgin"? (*She leaves the paper on the table. She rises and crosses to Marie-Thérèse*) Doubts such as yours, Mother Marie-Thérèse, are not easily overcome. I need not remind you that I am here not only as your superior but as your friend. And when they question you on the state of her soul— remember that the evidence is in your hands.

(*The* REVEREND MOTHER *goes out* L.
MARIE-THÉRÈSE *becomes aware of the exercise-book she is holding in her hand. She opens it and begins to read. As she sits there in the fading light, turning the pages, she is overcome by what she finds. In the distance the Lourdes Hymn can be heard*)

MARIE-THÉRÈSE. Were you a martyr, Bernadette? Tortured in mind and body over twenty years? Because, one day, as a child, you walked by the Gave and talked for a few brief moments among the rocks and stones with the very Mother of God herself? (*Suddenly she closes the book with a vigorous action and places it on the corner of the table*) Dear God, what a price to pay for grace! Or was it? I don't know. I still don't know. Must I spend all my days struggling to understand?

(*Exercising all her tremendous self-control she pulls herself together, rises, and leaves the room. Only the book remains in a little pool of light from the lamp*)

The CURTAIN *falls*

PROPERTY AND FURNITURE PLOT

ACT I

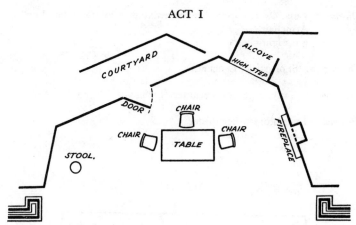

On stage : Table
  3 chairs
  Stool
  Stove. *On it :* pot of soup, can of hot water
    Beside it : linen airing
  Bundle of bedding
  On mantelpiece : half-loaf of bread, 4 soup bowls, lamp

Off stage : Clean laundry (LOUISE)

Personal : LOUISE: shawl
  FRANCOIS: coins
  LOUIS: stick
  BERNADETTE: basket of sticks

ACT II

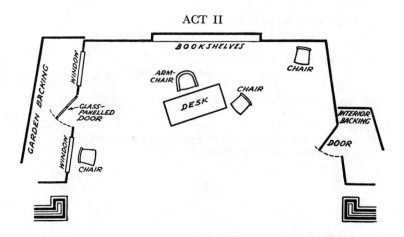

On stage: Desk. *On it:* papers, breviary, statuette, inkstand, hand bell
            Armchair
            3 upright chairs

Off stage R: Short stick (LECLERC)

Off stage L: Tray, 2 glasses, decanter (LECLERC)

Personal: LECLERC: feather duster
            LACADÉ: watch
            LOUIS: stick

ACT III

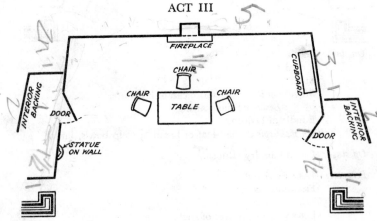

On stage: Table. *On it:* pen and ink, heap of linen, Infirmary record
            3 chairs
            Medicine cupboard
            Statue

Off stage R: Doves (MARIE-RAPHAEL)
            Note-book, lamp (REVEREND MOTHER)

Off stage L: Box of bandages, etc.; tissue paper inside (MARIE-VERON-
            IQUE)

Personal: MARIE-THÉRÈSE: letter, rosary, bundle of linen
            MARIE-RAPHAEL: rosary

LIGHTING PLOT

ACT I

Property fittings required: 1 portable lamp

THE APPARENT SOURCES OF LIGHT are a window (unseen), and later the portable lamp

THE MAIN ACTING AREAS cover the whole set

Late afternoon, in February

To open: *Fade in single spot to light Reverend Mother's face only*   **(Page 1)**

Cue 1   REVEREND MOTHER: "... How easy it would be to
         understand."   **(Page 1)**
         Quick fade of spot

Cue 2   As soon as Reverend Mother has cleared   **(Page 1)**
         Fade in general lighting on Cachot
         Bright sunlight outside door

Cue 3   Bernadette appears in the doorway   **(Page 9)**
         Very slow check of sunlight outside

Cue 4   Louis exits   **(Page 17)**
         Start slow fade of stage lighting
         Light outside door changes from day to night

Cue 5   Louise puts lamp on table   **(Page 17)**
         Increase light round table, check remainder

Cue 6   Louise moves lamp to mantelpiece   **(Page 20)**
         Bring up light round fireplace and LC

Cue 7   LACADÉ: "Don't play the innocent with me ..."
         He moves down L   **(Page 21)**
         Slight check of lights brought up in Cue 5

ACT II

Property fittings required: none

THE APPARENT SOURCES OF LIGHT are windows in the R wall

THE MAIN ACTING AREAS cover desk and areas immediately R and L of it and below it

Morning, in March

To open: *Bright sunlight through windows*

No cues

ACT III

Property fittings required: 1 portable lamp

  The Apparent Sources of Light are a window in the fourth wall

  The Main Acting Areas cover the table and the areas below it and
   RC and LC

To open: *Cold daylight*

Cue 1 Marie-Thérèse: "Do you recognize this?" (Page 58)
   Slight slow check of light round edges of room, leaving
    light round the table slightly more accentuated

Cue 2 Marie-Thérèse: "Teach me to be sure. Show me." (Page 60)
   Quick fade to Black-Out

Cue 3 As Marie-Veronique enters (Page 60)
   Quick fade up to general lighting, now a little warmer and
    less bright than the opening

Cue 4 Marie-Raphael hastens off L (Page 66)
   Slow fade to leave pool round table at Marie-Thérèse's exit

Cue 5 Bernadette: ". . . My rosary . . ." (Page 67)
   Quick fade to Black-Out

Cue 6 Reverend Mother enters with lamp and comes to
   table (Page 68)
   Bring up soft lights round table

Cue 7 Marie-Thérèse leaves the room (Page 70)
   Fade out all lights except spot on book

EFFECTS PLOT

ACT I

Cue 1   As the CURTAIN rises   **(Page 1)**
Fade in Lourdes Hymn, bringing up volume and fading away to simulate passing procession

Cue 2   LOUISE: ". . . Perhaps her aunt would have her again . . ."   **(Page 20)**
Confused voices outside door

Cue 3   LACADE: ". . . You wait here."   **(Page 20)**
Hammering at door

ACT II

Cue 1   As the CURTAIN rises   **(Page 23)**
Door bell

Cue 2   LECLERC: ". . . I'm coming."   **(Page 23)**
Door bell

Cue 3   LECLERC: ". . . the devil to pay."   **(Page 23)**
Door bell

ACT III

Cue 1   . . . she stares at Bernadette unable to answer the truth of this   **(Page 59)**
Handbell

Cue 2   MARIE-THÉRÈSE: ". . . would help me to see better."   **(Page 67)**
Bell

Cue 3   Bernadette sinks to the floor   **(Page 67)**
Bell stops

Cue 4   As soon as the Lights have faded to blackness   **(Page 68)**
Minute bell
Dies Irae

Cue 5   Immediately before the Reverend Mother enters with the lamp   **(Page 68)**
Fade Dies Irae
Stop Bell

Cue 6   As Marie-Thérèse leaves the room   **(Page 70)**
Fade in softly Lourdes Hymn